3535
nw 58th

When Sparrows Fall

(For Sparrows Do Fall)

Kenneth Lay

CROSSBOOKS
PUBLISHING

CrossBooks™
1663 Liberty Drive
Bloomington, IN 47403
www.crossbooks.com
Phone: 1-866-879-0502

First published by CrossBooks 12/21/2009

ISBN: 978-1-6150-7112-8 (sc)
ISBN: 978-1-6150-7121-0 (hc)

Library of Congress Control Number: 2009943796

Printed in the United States of America
Bloomington, Indiana

This book is printed on acid-free paper.

Unless otherwise indicated, all Scripture references will be from the King James Version of the Bible. All other references will be designated as follows:
Beck—William F. Beck
ESV—English Standard Version
Gspd—Edgar J. Goodspeed
LB—The Living Bible
NIV—New International Version
TCNT—Twentieth Century New Testament

Dedicated To

My wife Anna, my family, my friends, and my God in appreciation
for their encouragement and prayers for me and my ministry.

Scripture

Matthew 10:29

"Are not two sparrows sold for a farthing? and one of them shall not fall on the ground without your Father."

...without your Father's permission—Beck
...can fall to the ground—Gspd
...without your Father's knowledge—TCNT

"Are not two sparrows sold for a penny? Yet not one of them will fall to the ground apart from the will of your Father....So don't be afraid; you are worth more than many sparrows."—NIV
Matthew 10:29, 30

Contents

Introduction

"When Sparrows Fall" is a personal journey along the road of suffering and sorrow. It engages the realities of life and focuses on the "unexplainables" of life, that is, the sorrows, disappointments, tragedies, and other uncontrollable events which do not turn out as we had hoped, and consequently do not have the proverbial "happy" ending.

Come with me on this journey through life. We shall take a realistic look at life and evaluate some of its experiences. We shall discover the kind of world in which we live and what to expect along the way. There are many travelers on this road and no man travels alone. All humanity walks here. Life, both good and bad, is lived on this road; however, life's journey need not be filled with despair nor consumed with sadness. There is hope! There is joy! And by the grace of God you can enjoy this incredible journey!

I have written these personal essays from the perspective of a son, a husband, a father and a grandfather. As a son, I experienced the death of my mother and father who died in the same fatal automobile accident. As a husband, I know what it means to see your wife suffer through a mastectomy due to cancer as well as a hysterectomy due to the same disease. As a father, I know the joy, the care and the concern of having children and hurting when they hurt, which, by the way does not lessen but rather intensifies as they grow older. As a grandfather, I know the joy of having healthy, intelligent grandchildren and seeing them grow to successful adulthood. I also know the heartache involved with the suffering and dying of a beautiful and intelligent granddaughter diagnosed with the terminal disease of cystic fibrosis.

So I present these personal essays for your consideration as you join me on this perplexing journey of suffering and sorrow through the years which ends, by the way, not in defeat but in victory!

--Kenneth Lay

CHAPTER ONE

A Sparrow Falls

The first sparrow to fall in my life fell on Christmas Day, 1938, when a cold, deep snow covered the ground, winter birds were foraging for food, and the sparrows had discovered the single pieces of grain which had fallen through the cracks in the trough where Dad fed the cattle.

They were so hungry and intent on eating the yellow grain that they did not notice the nine year old boy. I approached with my brand-new BB gun, "the Red Ryder", which I had just received that morning as a Christmas gift. With quiet, slow, measured steps I approached the feeding sparrows from the opposite side of the trough, so as to not attract their attention. Taking careful aim, I deliberately lowered the barrel of my gun over the edge of the trough until it was only a few inches from the head of one of the sparrows, and I slowly pulled the trigger.

In the quiet of the morning, to my ears, the noise of that first shot out of my new BB gun sounded like the blast of a cannon. All the sparrows quickly flew away, except one, which just lay there, lifeless. I stared at that small, still sparrow as a bright-red color began to stain the snow around its head. As I watched transfixed, it seemed that the ever widening stain would never stop. I stood there, not proud of my accomplishment, but saddened by the fall of the sparrow. Rather than being thrilled and excited as I had anticipated, I was deeply disturbed. Tears ran down my cheeks, I began to sob, and slowly turned and walked away, distressed and confused by my tearful response to what had just occurred.

As I entered the house, still crying, my observant, caring Mom, asked me what was wrong. I told her what I had done and how it had made me feel so sad that I just began to cry. She touched me as she wisely said the words which I have used throughout my lifetime, "Why don't you tell God about it and he will help you feel better." So I did, and miraculously He did! That was my introduction to a world where sparrows fall—for sparrows do fall.

The first sparrow, in my life, had fallen and little did I realize how many sparrows were yet to fall during my lifetime. They would fall on many different occasions—but fall they would! And with the fall of each sparrow, I would tell God all about it (a lesson learned early in life), and somehow he would make me feel better. Words of wisdom, graciously given by a loving mother, prepared me and enabled me to live in a world where sparrows fall—for sparrows do fall. However, above all else, this one thing I know, they do not fall without the awareness of a caring and compassionate God who loves us and wants us to know him as our Heavenly Father. Jesus said, "Are not two sparrows sold for a farthing (penny)? Yet, not one of them can fall to the ground without your Father, that is, without his knowledge and permission. Fear not therefore; you are of more value than many sparrows." (Matthew 10:29, 31 paraphrased).

The fall of this sparrow was my first close encounter with death, but it certainly would not be the last. Many friends and loved ones would die, and there would be multiple funerals to attend, the last of which would be my own. "For it is appointed unto man once to die." One thing I have learned, you cannot deal with death until it arrives. I thought I understood and had settled the issue of death until my parents were killed instantly in an automobile accident; but I came to realize you cannot deal with the fall of any sparrow until that sparrow falls. Death was dressed differently when it came for my granddaughter than it was when it came for my parents. Death is always dressed differently when it arrives whether it's coming for loved ones or friends or strangers, and I am sure it will be clothed differently when it comes for me. When it does finally arrive we recognize it for what it is, the end of life upon this earth but the beginning of the life to come.

We are never ready or prepared for the arrival of death no matter how many times it comes. We cannot react or embrace the event until it actually occurs. One may prepay his funeral expenses and purchase his tombstone, but he cannot "prepay" his response to death.

To help us understand the fall of that sparrow and the fall of other sparrows, I call your attention to the various factors which entered into the death of that first sparrow.

First of all, the human factor: My parents loved me and expressed that love by giving me an extra special BB gun, "the Red Ryder", as a gift for Christmas. That was the year the Red Ryder was first introduced by Daisy Outdoor Products. It is possibly the most famous BB gun in American history. My nine-year-old heart was thrilled beyond words to receive such a wonderful gift, and my childish mind began a process of imagination that enabled me to kill all kinds of game, both large and small.

Second, the natural process of life: Dad had already poured the welcome, daily feed for the cattle into the feed troughs and the eager hungry cows had eaten, with some of the seeds falling through the cracks down onto the snow. Always, after the cows had finished eating and left the troughs, the hungry winter birds, mainly sparrows, flew down to eat the leftover grain which lay upon the ground. This was a natural process which occurred on a daily basis during the winter.

Third, personal desire, choice, and action: Into this natural process I entered with my own personal desire and ambition—to shoot my new

3

BB gun and hopefully hit my target. Those factors and events which were totally innocent and natural, when joined together, resulted in the fall of that sparrow.

The reality that we live in a world where sparrows do fall, calls for the "why" question. It also calls for that question to be answered. However, the real question is not "Why do sparrows fall?" The answer to that question is quite simple; sparrows fall because that's the kind of world in which we live. The real question is "Why did my sparrow fall at this particular time and place?" The purpose of these personal experiences is to deal with that issue. Not that I shall answer the question to everybody's satisfaction, but that I shall share some thoughts which, hopefully, will enable you to come to terms with the fall of sparrows in your own life.

The answer to the "Why?" question is not as complicated as we have made it. In fact, it is very simple. The world in which we live demands that sparrows fall. We live in a "fallen" world. The circumstances of life and the desire of man coupled with his choices and actions answer the "Why?" question. It is within the framework of the natural process of life that sparrows fall.

Yes, that is a very simplistic answer to the "Why?" question, and from a humanistic standpoint that's all that is required. However, there is one other aspect we must consider in answering the question, "Why do sparrows fall?" That aspect is God! And when God enters the picture the answer is no longer simple. It becomes Divinely complicated.

Without God in the picture it was a simple matter of a mother and father giving their son a Christmas present, a new BB gun, the excitement of a young boy, the feeding of cattle, some hungry birds foraging for food, the snow covered earth, the determination of a boy to get close enough to the birds for a sure shot, and the pulling of the trigger. Result: one dead sparrow.

Should we place God in this picture? If not, it's just one dead sparrow, so move on to the next kill. However, we must introduce God into this picture because God introduced Himself into this "fallen" world when Jesus came and said, "Are not two sparrows sold for a farthing? And one of them shall not fall on the ground without your Father." (Matthew 10:29). So whether we recognize Him in the picture or not, God is there. Jesus put Him there!

Without God in the picture there is no basis for good or evil. Without God in the picture there is no explanation for life or death, sin or righteousness. Without God in the picture there is no explanation for our being and no ultimate purpose for our existence. It is at this point we must consider not only God but also the existence of sin and its consequences (suffering, pain, disease, murder, rape, all kinds of evil, and death). In the beginning, in this world where Adam and Eve lived and walked and talked with God, death did not exist, evil did not exist, sin did not exist, fear did not exist, pain did not exist, suffering did not exist and sparrows did not fall! Consequently, there was no stress, no grief, no sorrow, no heartache, and no crying, that is, until Adam and Eve ate the forbidden fruit. At that time sin entered this world and everything changed! Along with sin came suffering, disease, death, decay, etc. (Genesis 3:1-19), and now, all of those things are part and parcel of life as we know it. There is no escape from the effects of Adam's sin except through the provision which God made by sending his Son to deal with our sin.

The very root of suffering is found in the soil of sin. Had it not been for sin there would be no such thing as suffering, only bliss and perfect fellowship with the Father himself, such as Adam and Eve had in the Garden of Eden before they sinned by disobeying God and rejecting his authority. The God of the Bible is the only One who deals adequately with all the issues of life. According to God's Word all of those things which make men miserable, all the negatives of life, are the result of the rebellion of Adam and Eve in the Garden of Eden. It was there they rebelled against the authority of God, even after they had been warned of the consequence: death. "And the Lord God commanded the man, saying, Of every tree of the garden thou mayest freely eat; but of the tree of the knowledge of good and evil, thou shalt not eat of it, for in the day that thou eatest thereof thou shalt surely die." (Genesis 2:16-17) The day Adam and Eve disobeyed God and ate the forbidden fruit is the day sin, suffering, and death entered this world.

As a result of their rebellion we live in a diseased world, a sick world, morally, physically, and spiritually. Romans 5:12 reminds us that by one man sin entered into the world and death by sin; and so death passed upon all men for all have sinned. **Sin is the ultimate explanation for the fall of sparrows.** Without sin there would never have been such a thing as death, disease, hate, murder, adultery, rape, lying, stealing, or any of the other things that make life miserable for man.

We should rejoice that God injected himself into this picture of life and death. It is His presence at the funeral of a sparrow that gives us hope. It is in the context of God's awareness of the fall of a sparrow that Jesus said, "Not one sparrow (What do they cost? Two for a penny?) can fall to the ground without your Father knowing it. So don't worry! You are more valuable to him than many sparrows." (Matthew 10:29, 31 LB) God cares more about you than he does a whole flock of sparrows, yet he maintains a watch over each one of them as he also watches over you. Therein lies our hope when sparrows fall in our own life—for sparrows do fall.

With God in the picture something new has been added: Hope! With God in the picture there is hope, but without God there is no hope. Take God out of the picture and there is nothing left but a dead sparrow. Of course that does not answer the "Why?" question, but it does introduce a new dimension into the experience.

That sparrow fell because I chose to kill it. Most sparrows fall because of natural causes or the choice of a human being or a combination of both; however, there is one other cause for the fall of sparrows in our own life. We call it "the will of God", or "the sovereignty of God", or "predestination", or "foreknowledge". When God is in the picture there are "unexplainables" to consider. God himself is unexplainable.

Who can know the mind of God? Who can understand his ways? Who can reconcile such contrasting truths as "the sovereignty of God" and "the free will of man"?

Listen to Isaiah as he speaks God's words, "This plan of mine is not what you would work out, neither are my thoughts the same as yours! For just as the heavens are higher than the earth, so are my ways higher than yours, and my thoughts than yours." (Isaiah 55: 8-9 LB) Listen as Paul exclaims, "Oh, what a wonderful God we have! How great are his wisdom and knowledge and riches! How impossible it is for us to understand his decisions and his methods! For who among us can know the mind of the Lord? Who knows enough to be his counselor and guide?" (Romans 11:33-34 LB). We must leave the imponderables and "unexplainables" with God. That requires a choice! To choose faith, and trust in a loving, caring, compassionate, all-wise, and all-powerful God. With the fall of each sparrow we rest our case on the character of God.

"Are not two sparrows sold for a farthing? and one of them shall not fall on the ground without your Father.—Fear ye not therefore, ye are of more value than many sparrows." (Matthew 10:29, 31) To know that our Heavenly Father is always aware of what is happening in our lives should relieve fear and replace it with hope and peace.

There are those who, for whatever reason, prefer to keep God out of the picture. They are uncomfortable with such a God as the Bible presents. They are not averse to people having gods; they are only opposed to the God of the Bible, the God who became flesh and dwelt among men and is known as Jesus Christ. Even though some men have tried to erase God from the pages of history and the minds of other men, he remains. No man can eliminate God. They can try to ignore him and pretend that he does not exist, but even in the process of doing so, they admit that he is. Otherwise, why try to deny or ignore or pretend that something that doesn't exist does not really exist?

On the other hand if we believe God does exist and that he is who the Bible says he is, then we must tell others the good news that in and through Jesus Christ there is Hope! There is Hope when a sparrow falls! There is Hope when a child dies! There is Hope when a spouse leaves! There is Hope when a disease strikes! There is Hope when a business fails! The emphasis is no longer upon the fall of the sparrow—for sparrows do fall. The emphasis now is upon God and his awareness of the sparrow's fall and his reassuring words "Fear not, you are of more value than many sparrows." Yes, with God in the picture, there is Hope!

Back to the "Why?" question: Sparrows fall because of natural causes, someone's personal choice, the will of God (either sovereign or permissive), or a combination of all three. My first sparrow fell because of my personal choice, a choice which I later regretted.

In considering the various causes for the fall of certain sparrows, listen to these words in Luke 13:1-5 LB: "About this time he (Jesus) was informed that Pilate had butchered some Jews from Galilee as they were sacrificing at the Temple in Jerusalem. 'Do you think they were worse sinners than other men from Galilee?' he asked. 'Is that why they suffered? Not at all! And don't you realize that you also will perish unless you leave your evil ways and turn to God? And what about the eighteen men who died when the Tower of Siloam fell on them? Were they the worst sinners in Jerusalem? Not at all! And you, too, will perish unless you repent.'"

Consider one other incident in the life of Jesus as you seek the answer to the "Why?" question of fallen sparrows: "As he went along, he saw a man blind from birth. His disciples asked him, 'Rabbi, who sinned, this man or his parents, that he was born blind?' 'Neither this man nor his parents sinned,' said Jesus, 'but this happened so that the work of God might be displayed in his life.'" (John 9:1-3 NIV)

Also consider the fact that some sparrows fall as the direct result of God's permission, as in Job's case! As a result of God giving Satan permission to test Job, tragedy struck! Sparrows fell in every area of Job's life. He lost his family, he lost his servants, he lost his cattle, he lost his camels, he lost his sheep, and finally he lost his health! (Job 1:1-2:7).

We should not sit in judgment on the misfortunes of others, as did Job's friends. Their assumptions were all wrong as to the cause of Job's suffering. There are just too many variables as to the "Why?" of such things. In fact, we should even be careful about blaming ourselves for something bad that has happened. We should not sit in judgment on our own misfortunes and certainly not on the misfortunes of others. Of course, if the Holy Spirit convicts us that what has happened to us is the result of our own sin, we should ask God to forgive us and if necessary ask others to forgive us. We should also forgive ourselves, stop "beating ourselves to death" for it, stop brooding about it, and get on with living the abundant life which God wants us to live.

What cause would you assign those who were butchered by Pilate, the eighteen killed by the fall of the Tower of Siloam, and the man who was born blind? In trying to answer the question, "Why?", it will always help to keep in mind that sometimes sparrows fall through no fault of their own; sometimes they fall by their own hand; but sometimes they fall by the hand of another, such as a drinking driver, a driver on drugs, a terrorist, a thief, a murderer, etc. Unfortunately sparrows also fall at the hand of nature itself, such as floods, earthquakes, tornadoes, diseases, etc. Sparrows fall for various reasons—but they do fall! Therefore, thank God for the Hope through Jesus Christ!

CHAPTER TWO

An Epidemic Strikes

During my senior year in High School, in 1947, the Holy Spirit began to impress upon my heart that I should preach the Word of God and be the pastor of a church, and that impression continued to grow until it became a conviction that would not go away.

Unable to come to terms with the "call to the ministry", after graduation I took a job as an accountant with a pipeline construction company which was laying a pipeline from Gainesville, Texas, to Humbolt, Kansas. At the conclusion of that job I decided to become a salesman for Tayloe Paper Company in Tulsa, Oklahoma. It was while working there the conviction that I should preach became a very real and heavy burden, a burden which I could not lay down. In response, I gave the company a two-week notice and enrolled in Oklahoma Baptist University in Shawnee, Oklahoma, to further pursue God's will for my life.

In 1950, I married my high school sweetheart, Anna, and a few months later the First Baptist Church of Prue, Oklahoma, called me to be their pastor and ordained me to preach the Gospel. In addition to my class work, I worked a forty hour week at Humpty Dumpty

Supermarket, and drove one hundred twenty miles to the church to preach on Sundays.

Anna and I had been married for two years when the polio epidemic, which was rampant in America, struck the small community of Prue. The dreaded disease had spread like a wild fire, sweeping throughout the country, and it ravaged the community of Prue. As a pastor, I tried to visit those who were afflicted with the disease, and in the process contracted it myself.

Out of a population of 120, Prue had thirteen hospitalized cases of polio, and I was one of those thirteen. Being struck down by the disease, poliomyelitis, for which there was no known cure, was the second sparrow to fall in my life. The polio epidemic was like a tsunami, leaving in its wake thousands of individuals who died, along with thousands of others with crippled bodies, bodies no longer able to function as they once did. Since there were not enough rooms available in the hospital, some lay on makeshift cots and beds in the hallways. With various nerve and muscle functions gone, some temporary but many permanently, most patients were paralyzed unable to move their limbs, feed themselves or turn over in bed.

Other victims of the disease lay immobile in "iron lungs", a large cylindrical machine into which the entire body, except the head, was placed. The function of the machine was to breathe for the victim, taking the place of their lungs which no longer functioned because of the effects of polio. The fortunate victims were those who were able to breathe on their own and were able to move about with the aid of a wheelchair or braces and crutches.

The polio "virus" attacked the nerves responsible for muscular movements. If the nerves were completely destroyed it was just a matter of time until the muscles began to atrophy; consequently, the arm or leg became smaller and weaker. At some point the nerves in that area, which were not completely dead, began to take over and "talk" to the muscles that remained and the process of deterioration stabilized. That which had been lost could never be regained, but what was left could be strengthened to some degree.

Some of those in the iron lungs recovered enough "lung power" to remain outside the iron lung with a chest respirator for a short period of time before they had to re-enter. Some were able to escape the iron lung completely, but many did not survive.

At one point I was totally helpless, unable to move my arms and legs, but fortunately, because my lungs had not been affected, I was able to breathe on my own. After a few weeks of intense therapy I was able to feed myself. A short time later I could be lifted out of the bed, placed in a wheelchair by a hospital nurse or volunteer who would take me on a "joy-ride". Sometimes when I was feeling particularly sorry for myself they would roll me down to the iron lung section so I could see how blessed I was not to be there. Those rides always enabled me to adjust my perspective.

When the doctors finally concluded that the disease had run its course (for they had no way of stopping it) it was time for rehabilitation. What had been more or less a waiting game now became an aggressive fight toward recovery. The nerves and muscles which were not affected by the virus had to be retrained and strengthened to carry the load of those which had been destroyed; however, before this could take place all the muscles had to be stretched back to their normal length, as much as possible. Due to the type of prior treatment (lying on a "bed board" flat on the stomach or back) the muscles tightened up from lack of use; consequently, they had to be stretched back to normal elasticity.

This effort at rehabilitation consisted of heat treatments (also known as Sister Kenny Wrap because she invented it) along with stretching and movement exercises. The heat treatment was achieved by wrapping the total body in woolen army blankets which had been soaked in hot water. On top of this was laid a sheet of plastic to help retain the heat. It was believed the heat would loosen the rigid nerves and muscles and make the stretching easier and more effective. After the heat treatment, we were taken downstairs to the "torture" room or the "dungeon" which is what we called the therapy room. There they laid us on our back with our legs straight out flat in front of us. As one therapist stood at our feet while holding our hands and pulling and two more stood on either side of us with their hands under our shoulders pushing upwards, they unmercifully stretched the back, buttocks, leg, and arm muscles. The ultimate goal was to enable us to sit upright on the table with our legs flat in front of us. The pain was excruciating and it was always with fearful anxiety and trepidation that we went to therapy each day. We knew what was coming, and the closer we got to the room the greater the dread because we would hear the screaming and crying of those already there.

Finally the rehabilitation was finished, and after a stay of three months I was dismissed from the hospital to continue therapy on my own for a period of two years. The theory being that therapy would accomplish all it was going to within a period of two years. When I left the hospital I was in a wheelchair and had a brace on my right hand. After a few months I graduated from the wheelchair to a set of Everett canes (special crutches) and a knee-high metal and leather brace on my left leg.

After I was admitted to the hospital Anna withdrew both of us from Oklahoma Baptist University and went to work in the Pathology Department of the Oklahoma School of Medicine typing autopsy reports, of all things! Anna's parents and some of my family moved our possessions from Shawnee to a little house they had found and rented in Oklahoma City. The church at Prue continued to pay my salary ($15.00 a week), and the Delaware-Osage Baptist Association paid the interim preacher's salary. This support, along with Anna's job, made it possible for us to live in Oklahoma City the year of my hospitalization and recuperation. As soon as I regained enough strength I returned to preaching at Prue. The following year, after being dismissed from the hospital, we returned to Shawnee to finish our last semester of college.

From the beginning of the polio attack it never occurred to either of us that I would never get back to "normal". We did not play the "what if" game. What if I die? What if I never get out of the hospital? What if I can never work again? What if we cannot finish college or go on to the Seminary? I do not recall any of those questions being asked. Anna may have worried about those things, but if she did she never mentioned it. I think we both just assumed that God would take care of us. We did finish college and went on to Southwestern Baptist Theological Seminary in Fort Worth, Texas, from which we both received our degrees.

After corrective surgery while in Fort Worth, the brace on my right hand was no longer necessary. Some months later I was able to walk without the crutches, and after several years I was able to walk without the leg brace; however, later in life I had to return to wearing a leg brace.

My involvement with polio was the second sparrow which fell in my life. As I think back to those days, I realize that had it not been for the sufficiency of God's grace that experience could have brought about the end of my ministry as well as the end of our marriage. I know now that difficult times do one of two things: they either make your faith stronger or they destroy it; they either make your marriage stronger or they destroy it. Fortunately, in our case, it served to deepen our love and appreciation for each other and did not lessen our commitment to serve God.

By God's grace and purpose for my life I was far more than I could ever be otherwise, and because of Anna's love and encouragement I never gave up even though there were times when I wanted to. I'm sure there must have been times when she wanted to as well, but God's grace and purpose prevailed.

When you face difficult times you have to face the truth about yourself and your faith. You have to answer the question: Who am I? Although I knew it from the beginning, the answer was solidified in my mind and heart: I was a man who had to be totally dependent upon God. That is not to say that I was more committed to God than any other man, but it is to say that my need for Divine assistance was total in every area of my life, especially preaching. The promise God gave me to carry me through my college years was Proverbs 3:5-6, "Trust in the Lord with all thine heart; and lean not unto thy own understanding. In all thy ways acknowledge him and he shall direct thy paths."

William Shakespeare had it right when he said, "There's a special providence in the fall of a sparrow." There comes a time in every man's life, and for me there were many, when he must turn everything over to God in total trust. In fact, total trust in God is the absolute and only way to live life on a daily basis. That means being able to say from both heart and mind what Paul wrote in II Timothy 1:12 "I know whom I have believed and am persuaded that he is able to keep that which I have committed unto him against that day." That means to pray a prayer which I have often prayed: "Father, I have given you my life, my soul, my health, my family, my ministry, my finances, my material possessions, everything, and I trust you with it all." Truly, God has proven to be a good steward of all I have entrusted to him.

In light of all that, you may think it strange and somewhat disappointing for me to say that life does not come with a "satisfaction guaranteed" warranty. There are no refunds in life. There are no guarantees, not even for Christians. You must live life as it comes. If you think being a Christian guarantees you a life of health, wealth, and happiness you are greatly mistaken. If you think being a Christian guarantees that things will always work out the way you want them to, or expect them to, or think they should, you are in for some real disappointments. On the other hand, if you believe God loves you, is always with you, and will sustain you no matter what comes, you will never be without hope.

When sparrows fall, for sparrows do fall, you must keep in mind that sorrow, sickness, disease, death, tragedy, abnormalities, murders, rapes, robberies, wars, and natural disasters are all part of life. Any or all of those things may come into anyone's life, at any given time, Christian or not. We must face the reality of life. This is just the way things are on this earth and in this fallen world where we live. In fact, Jesus said, "In the world ye shall have tribulation." But that isn't all he said, he went on to say, "But be of good cheer, I have overcome the world." (John 16:33) In that same verse he said, "These things I have spoken unto you, that in me ye might have peace." Therein lies the basis for victorious Christian living. Jesus was victorious. He overcame the world. He is the Prince of Peace. On that basis we have reason to rejoice, even when sparrows fall. John said it this way, "For whatsoever is born of God overcometh the world and this is the victory that overcometh the world, even our faith. Who is he that overcometh the world, but he that believeth that Jesus is the Son of God?" (I John 5:4-5)

That kind of faith is victorious. It enables a person to live above the circumstances rather than under them. I heard of a man who said to his friend, "How are you?" and his friend replied, "OK, I guess, under the circumstances." Then the man replied, "What are you doing under the circumstances? Get above them!" Regardless of the circumstances God is still in control! "Be of good cheer, I have overcome the world." The implication is, you can too!

When facing the realities of life the world will respond one way and the true believer, that person who has committed himself to God in total trust and obedience, will respond another. To be sure, there are similarities in all of our responses when it comes time to face the negative realities of life: despair, depression, denial, hopelessness, anger, disillusion, tears, silence, withdrawal, fantasies, etc., but the believer goes beyond all of those initial responses. He does not stay in that defeated state of mind, he goes through and beyond it, and he goes to God, the God of hope.

The Psalmist wrote, "Why art thou cast down, O my soul? and why art thou disquieted in me? hope thou in God: for I shall yet praise him for the help of his countenance." (Psalm 42:5) Faith calls for hope. Hope calls for confidence, confidence that God makes a difference even in the midst of our sorrows and disappointments. The Apostle

Paul, through all of his adverse circumstances, learned an important lesson which he shared with us in Philippians 4:11, "I have learned, in whatsoever state I am, therewith to be content." Faith, hope, and confidence in God lead to contentment regardless of the circumstances. When sparrows fall, "Hope thou in God"! We must see God at work when sparrows fall for "We know that in everything God works...!" (Romans 8:28 Gspd)

In our humanity we tend to abandon hope right at the very time we need it most. Our tendency is to "give in" to the circumstances rather than resist them with hope and confidence in God. We allow the circumstances to dictate our emotions during trying times instead of allowing faith and hope in God to lift our spirits and enable us to "rise above" our circumstances. To be sure, it is difficult to have peace in the midst of the storm, but that is exactly the time faith and hope should reign supreme!

We talk about peace in the midst of the storm. What is peace? Some people think peace is the absence of conflict, or confrontation, or sickness, or failure, or turmoil or any other kind of difficulty. However, being at peace does not mean the absence of problems; being happy does not mean the absence of sorrow; being joyful does not mean the absence of disappointment; being content does not mean the absence of conflict. The Holy Spirit living in the believer is the One who produces love, joy, and peace even in the midst of all kinds of adversities.

Others think peace is dependent upon circumstances. But that is the world's concept of peace. The peace which the world gives is dependent upon circumstances, whereas the peace which Jesus gives is dependent upon Him. He gives his peace in the midst of circumstances whether they are good or bad! Real genuine peace is not dependent upon the circumstances of life but upon the Giver of Life, Jesus himself.

Jesus spoke to this issue in John 14:27: "Peace I leave with you, my peace I give unto you: not as the world giveth, give I unto you. Let not your heart be troubled, neither let it be afraid." The peace which Jesus gives is in contrast to the peace which the world gives. The world's peace is fleeting and dependent upon circumstances or things; whereas the peace offered by Jesus is permanent and dependent upon him and him alone. I encourage you to read this poem reflectively.

PEACE IN THE MIDST OF THE STORM

When the world that I've been living in collapses at my feet,
When my life is shattered and torn,
Tho' I'm windswept and battered I can cling to His cross,
And find peace in the midst of my storm!

There is peace in the midst of my storm tossed life'
Oh, there's an Anchor, there's a Rock to build my faith upon.
Jesus rides in my vessel – so I'll fear no alarm.
He gives me peace in the midst of my storm!
--------Author Unknown

Although life, at times, is difficult, with God's help you can handle it! "Hope thou in God!" for he is the one who can alter the outcome of your circumstances and bring the peace that passes understanding.

CHAPTER THREE

A Car Wreck

At Bill's Corner near Stillwater, Oklahoma, an eighteen year old boy driving recklessly at an excessive speed, ran a stop sign, broadsided the car in which my mother and father were passengers, careened off of a telephone pole, and crashed into the middle gasoline pump of the store on the other side of the highway. My parents were killed instantly. My brother-in-law, who was driving the car, died a few days later. My sister was hospitalized for several weeks with severe injuries, some of which remained with her for the rest of her life. They were driving from Hominy, Oklahoma, where they lived, to Oklahoma City to visit me while I was in Crippled Children's' Hospital where all polio patients in that area were admitted for treatment.

That afternoon as I was slipping in and out of sleep while undergoing a Sister Kenny treatment, I heard the commentator on my roommate's radio say, "...a car wreck at Bill's corner...the Lays were sixty-two." I wasn't sure what I had heard, and it wasn't until my brothers and sisters arrived at my bedside that night that I knew for sure what had happened, and that both my mother and father had been killed in that wreck. That day, two sparrows fell in my life—for sparrows do fall.

The medical staff discussed whether or not I should attend my parent's funeral considering my paralysis, the physical weakness of my body, and the effect it might have upon my ongoing recovery. Their decision was that I could do so providing I remain on a stretcher at all times, and that I pay for a registered nurse to accompany me as well as pay for the ambulance. Of course I could do neither. The social worker at the hospital began making calls and one of the nurses volunteered to accompany me, and a used-car dealer provided, without cost, a driver and a car with a reclining seat. The ambulance service at Hominy had a gurney (stretcher) waiting for me upon my arrival.

Traveling from Oklahoma City to Hominy for the funeral service, I remember looking out the window as the cars drove by, and thinking that none of those people in the cars knew about my loss and sorrow. My mother and father were dead; my world was shattered; but outside that window it was business as usual. I wanted to shout to the world, "Stop! Look at me! I'm hurting!" I wanted the rest of the world to stop and mourn with me; however, that isn't the way it works. The world carries on with its usual activities unaware of the hurt and sorrow in the lives of those who have experienced the fall of a sparrow.

On the other hand, when I arrived at the church for the funeral service I was astonished to see that it was not only completely full, but people were standing outside on both sides of the building. As they carried me on the stretcher through all those people, including some of my family, it was then I realized that those who did know about my sorrow really cared. In addition to all those people I could see, there was someone else there I could not see: Jesus. If he is always present at the death of a sparrow, why would he not be there at the funeral of my loved ones? Did he not say, "Are not two sparrows sold for a penny? Yet not one of them will fall to the ground apart from the will of your Father....So don't be afraid; you are worth more than many sparrows." (Matthew 10:29, 31 NIV) I knew Jesus was there weeping with me, as he did with Mary and Martha at the grave of Lazarus. He feels every sorrow, he knows every pain, he sees every tear, and he is there.

At the conclusion of the funeral service I was not allowed to go to the cemetery for the burial, but was returned directly to the hospital in Oklahoma City. During the next several days I received many sympathy cards, but one card in particular (from an elderly saint in my parent's church) remains in my memory, not the printed portion but the handwritten words: "God in his power could have prevented it; but in his wisdom he did not!" Those words kept floating around in my mind until they finally lodged in my heart and produced a peace that passes all understanding. I have repeated those words on many occasions in my lifetime of ministry.

Two sparrows fell that day, my mother and my father, and not one of them fell without my Heavenly Father's knowledge and permission. He knew and he cared. Can you accept that and be comforted by it? Can you find a solace in simply knowing and believing that God knows and God cares?

"God in his power could have prevented it, but in his wisdom he did not!" The normal human reaction is to ask, "But why didn't He prevent it?" That was the charge, so to speak, that Mary and Martha brought against Jesus when their brother, Lazarus, died: "Lord, if you had been here, my brother would not have died." The implication being, "You could have prevented my brother's death. Why didn't you?"

Why didn't God prevent that car wreck? Why did he permit that collision which took three precious lives and left another to suffer not only the physical effects of that wreck but also the emotional scars which came with it? On the other hand, why didn't God prevent the suffering and death of his own Son? I came to realize it was "in his wisdom" and because of his great love for us. "For God so loved the world, that he gave his only begotten Son, that whosoever believeth in him should not perish, but have everlasting life." (John 3:16) There is also another reason; there was no other way He could deal with the sin-problem of humanity. Do you recall Jesus' prayer in the Garden of Gethsemane? "O my Father, if it be possible, let this cup pass from me: nevertheless not as I will, but as thou wilt—O my Father, if this cup may not pass away from me, except I drink it, thy will be done." (Matthew 26:39, 42) His suffering was necessary, absolutely essential, if we were to be forgiven and inherit eternal life!

God refused to "step in" from a distance and deal with our sin; but he did "step into" our humanity and deal with our sin in a very personal way. And even though he did not "step in" from a distance to prevent that life altering accident, he did "step in" in a very personal way and dealt with our sorrow.

Sometime after the funeral God gave me a very precious promise: "Fear thou not; for I am with thee: be not dismayed; for I am thy God: I will strengthen thee; yea, I will help thee; yea, I will uphold thee with the right hand of my righteousness." (Isaiah 41:10) Until this day I have claimed that as my favorite verse of Scripture. That promise of God's presence, help, and strength has carried me through the fall of every sparrow in my life. With the fall of each sparrow, the sorrow is there, the pain is there, the sense of loss is there, the questions are there, the deep hurt is there, and the tears are there; but so is God, so is his presence, so is his help, so is his strength, so is Jesus, so is his Holy Spirit, so is his comfort.

My brothers and sisters, desiring to erect a marker to identify our parents' grave, requested I suggest an appropriate Scripture to be engraved on the stone. Remembering what our father had said on one occasion, "Boys, I've given you a good name. Keep it that way." I selected Proverbs 22:1: "A good name is rather to be chosen than great riches." Our parents did have a good reputation and were well respected in the community. In conjunction with this a familiar Scripture comes to mind: "Honor thy father and thy mother." That commandment is still in effect even after the death of one's parents, and they can be honored by respecting their memory and living a life that reflects the character and reputation they enjoyed in the community where they lived.

My dad had always said that he did not want to die in debt to anyone, and without knowing it, he fulfilled that prophetic desire. The week before they were killed Dad had gone to each store in town where he had credit (this was before the days of credit cards) and paid every bill in full!

Dad did one other prophetic thing that morning before they left for Oklahoma City. The "bottom" had dropped out of the cattle market the day before, and he wanted to lift the spirits of my brother, who was partner with him in the cattle business, so just as a joke, he went out into the pasture and found a skeleton of the head of a cow, took it to the house and hung it on the gate-post with this note attached: "One cowman gone but not forgotten." When my brother heard the news that our parents were killed, he drove to their house. When he arrived, and got out of the car and walked up to the gate to open it, he saw that skeleton of the cow's head hanging there with the note attached: "One cowman gone but not forgotten."

Previously I mentioned the Scriptural promise (Isaiah 41:10) God had given me to strengthen me and help me deal with their death. He also gave my brother a Scriptural encouragement, Psalm 27:10 "When my father and my mother forsake me, then the Lord will take me up." Our Heavenly Father does not leave his children to face grief alone. He is with them. He is present at the fall and funeral of every sparrow. The word of God to Israel in Isaiah 43:1-5 (LB) is very comforting and encouraging to the believer when he is in the midst of life's difficulties. "---the Lord who created you, O Israel, says, Don't be afraid, for I have ransomed you; I have called you by name; you are mine. When you go through deep waters and great trouble, I will be with you. When you go through rivers of difficulty, you will not drown! When you walk through the fire of oppression, you will not be burned up—the flames will not consume you. For I am the Lord your God, your Savior, the Holy One of Israel. -----Don't be afraid, for I am with you."

Notice the operative word, "when", not "if" but "when": when you go through deep waters; when you go through rivers; when you walk through the fire. If you listen you can hear the graduating seriousness of the situation: waters, rivers, fire. When you pass through these things

25

the promise is, "I will be with you; they shall not overflow you; you will not be inundated; you will not be burned, consumed, or destroyed." Notice another operative word, "through". You do get through the threatening times and God is with you through it all.

God is faithful. You can count on him. You can sing with the hymn writer and praise God for forgiveness, pardon, peace and the faithfulness of God: "Pardon for sin and a peace that endureth, thine own dear presence to cheer and to guide; strength for today and bright hope for tomorrow, Blessings all mine, with ten thousand beside! Great is thy faithfulness! Great is thy faithfulness! Morning by morning new mercies I see; all I have needed thy hand hath provided; great is thy faithfulness, Lord, unto me!" (Words: Thomas O. Chisholm; Music: William M. Runyan)

When sparrows fall—for sparrows do fall, you cry, you mourn, you grieve; but somewhere in the midst of all that you begin to ask questions such as: What now? What next? How am I going to deal with this? How am I going to live life from this point forward? How can I deal with this tragedy effectively and victoriously?

What makes life worth living after all? The answer is GOD! I believe God and God alone makes life worth living. If all material possessions and every loved one were taken away, would life still be worth living? I believe it would. There comes a time and times in every man's life when all he has left is hope, hope in God. The Psalmist said to himself, "Take courage, my soul! ----Why then be downcast? Why be discouraged and sad? Hope in God!" (Psalm 42:4-5 LB). Listen to Habakkuk 3:17-19 LB: "Even though the fig trees are all destroyed, and there is neither blossom left nor fruit, and though the olive crops all fail, and the fields lie barren; even if the flocks die in the fields and the cattle barns are empty, yet I will rejoice in the Lord; I will be happy in the God of my salvation. The Lord God is my Strength, and he will give me the speed of a deer and bring me safely over the mountains."

As the hurt of the heart subsides, the sufficient grace of God begins to emerge. Embrace it! Cling to it! Lean on it! In the process of working though your loss and realizing that life will never be the same again, make the necessary adjustments in your lifestyle and in your emotions. Change what you can and accept what you cannot change. Acceptance is the key. Relinquish your sorrow to your Heavenly Father, who attends the funeral of every sparrow, who sees every tear that falls, who garners each tear drop and places it in his bottle and records each tear in his book of remembrance. Say with the Psalmist: "You alone are my God; my times are in your hands." (Psalm 31:15 LB)

CHAPTER FOUR

Two Surgeries

"CANCER", the most feared word in the medical vocabulary, if not for everyone at least for the patient. Back in 1977, for the doctor to say, "Your wife has cancer." was like hearing a judge pronounce the sentence of death.

For several months Anna, my wife, was concerned about a lump in her breast; however, the doctor continued to assure her that there was no need for concern. Not being comfortable with his advice, she even had a mammogram which, according to the technician and doctor, was negative. As the lump continued to increase in size her apprehension grew and became so strong she discussed it with our daughter, Susan, an RN. Susan said, "Mom, go see Dr. Hale. If it's there he will find it." After a thorough examination and discussing with her the length of time involved and the increasing size of the lump, the doctor suggested a biopsy with testing for malignancy.

Since we were concerned, we readily agreed to the doctor's recommendation for what we hoped was a minor procedure. The technician and surgeon both said, "It is probably nothing but we need to see". I was in the waiting room while the procedure was taking place. Due to the short length of time I was waiting, when the doctor came into the room to give me the report, I expected him to say, "Everything went well, the lump looks benign. There's nothing to worry about." Instead, he said, "We did the biopsy and had immediate testing. Your wife has breast cancer. You have two choices; you can take her home and schedule a mastectomy as soon as possible or have me proceed with the surgery right now."

Needless to say, I was stunned. I think my emotions and my mind shut down temporarily. I stared at him for a moment or two before I could think of anything to say. I finally said, "If it were your wife what would you do?" He replied, "If she were my wife I would remove the breast immediately. It must be done and the longer you wait the more the cancer will spread and the more invasive the surgery will be in order to remove the cancerous tissue. Besides that, she is already under the anesthesia and it will be less traumatic for her than waiting and having to undergo anesthesia again." It was most disturbing to have to make such a decision. How could I make that decision for her? I didn't think I had the right to do so, yet, at the same time, for her sake, I knew I had to make it. So I told him to perform the necessary surgery.

When Anna began to regain consciousness she asked the nurse "Is it over?", and the nurse replied, rather matter of factly, "Yes, honey, they removed your right breast." Then seeing the look on Anna's face the nurse said, "Oh, my God, you didn't know?" Anna's only thought before she slipped back into unconsciousness was, "I have cancer!"

The two days that followed were, for her, days of hovering between consciousness and unconsciousness as her body seemed to be trying to absorb the shock and pain. One night in particular her whole body continued to convulse, shudder and shake, trying to ward off the truth, so much so, that I tried to hold her down hard enough to stop the shaking, but to no avail. Finally, out of sheer exhaustion, her body went limp and she fell into a deep sleep. From that point forward she began to recover.

As a result of the surgery where they cut so deep and removed so much tissue, there almost wasn't enough flesh left to grow back together.

Three times they transplanted skin from another part of her body to enable the healing process to take place. It was very slow and painful but necessary in order to prevent infection and for healing to occur.

We discussed the physical effects of the surgery, but not much was said about the emotional effects. One of the major blessings was when the tests came back there was no invasion of the malignancy into the lymph nodes; therefore, the doctor did not think there was a need for chemotherapy or radiation.

The total effect of surgery and the shock of being told one of your breasts had been removed were not easy for her to overcome. I can not even imagine the traumatic impact of such an experience. Yet, Anna dealt with that issue as she dealt with every other difficult circumstance of life. She relied upon the promise and assurance provided by God in I Peter 5:7, (her favorite Scripture) "Casting all your care upon him for he careth for you." The Living Bible Paraphrased expands this verse to say, "Let him have all your worries and cares, for he is always thinking about you and watching everything that concerns you." The assurance that God cares for her enabled her to deal with the issue until she reached the point of acceptance. Years later, this same assurance carried her through a second bout of cancer which necessitated a hysterectomy. Once again, we were blessed with complete healing—"...He careth for you."

I have discovered that casting all your care upon God is not a once-in-a-lifetime matter. Rather, I have found it to be a daily necessity. The more difficult life becomes the more necessary it is to keep reminding yourself of God's caring and loving. Casting all your care upon God is a spiritual exercise that must be performed on a daily basis. So, when a sparrow falls, remember, God knows, God sees, and God cares. Take your burden to the Lord and leave it there.

The second surgery was mine. The symptoms leading up to my surgery developed rather slowly. They first began with a discomfort in my stomach which lasted for a couple of weeks. The discomfort was spasmodic at first then it became constant; it was the feeling of being full which turned into a feeling of being bloated. I did not feel like eating because I felt full constantly. The next stage of discomfort was the beginning of lower back pain. After a week or so the pain was almost unbearable and since Anna was sick with the flu, my daughter, Kendra, took me to the doctor's office. He examined me and told her to take me to the emergency room immediately and he would call and make arrangements for a surgeon to meet us there.

When I arrived at ER they did not wait to admit me, they sent me for X-rays at once. After the X-rays I was taken to a holding room. When they brought my X-rays in to show them to the doctor he looked at them and then asked me, "How did you get here?" I replied that I came by car. He said, "No, I mean did they bring you in on a gurney or in a wheelchair?" I said, "Neither, I walked in." The doctor said to the nurse, "These are not Mr. Lay's X-rays. He could not have walked in here in this condition." The nurse replied, "Doctor, those are his X-rays because I was with him when they were taken and they have not been out of my sight." He said to the nurse, "Re-schedule the rest of my surgeries, this man cannot wait."

Needless to say by this time I was becoming quite concerned and Kendra was crying. She called my wife and said, "Mom, they're taking Dad to surgery right now and he might have to have a colostomy." That's all I remember for the next several days, except sometime during those days I remember having a conversation with God. I remember thinking, "I believe I'll just go ahead and die." It was at that point the Lord said to me, "If that's what you want to do, it's alright. You can live or die which ever you prefer." I thought of my wonderful family and the thought of leaving them was not something I wanted to do, so I said, "In that case I want to live." I knew then I would recover.

I'm not sure how long it was until they told me all that had happened. The X-rays showed that I had a ruptured diverticulum, and my intestines had been leaking into the cavity of my abdomen for some time leading to peritonitis. The doctor removed twenty-six inches of my colon and performed a temporary colostomy. I had neither food nor drink for nine days until they heard bowel sounds and determined the surgery had been successful. They said at one point I was near death and my supposition is that was the point when I had my conversation with God. (Please understand that during this conversation I did not see anyone nor did I hear an audible voice; but the conversation was real nevertheless.) A few weeks after my first surgery, I returned to the hospital for the removal of the colostomy and the resectioning of my colon.

Except for this particular surgery and my bout with polio with its lingering effects I have enjoyed good health. I have known others who have suffered exceptionally. That raises some questions in my mind. Why is it that some people enjoy good health and others have to endure bad health? Is one a blessing and the other a curse? Is good health to be enjoyed and bad health to be resented? Is good health taken for granted or is it appreciated with gratitude by those who have it? Is good health guaranteed or is it temporary?

Why is it that some people are born with physical and mental impairments and others are born healthy? One person is born with every body part functioning properly while another person is born with parts of the body malformed and not functioning at all. Why is it that some people go through life without ever having to enter the hospital while others spend much of their life there? Some are stricken with disease at birth, some in their youth, some in their old age, and others never suffer at all.

Some abuse their health; others nurture it. The first are more likely to suffer severe pain, disease, and death; however, those who nurture their health are not immune to the same process. Each of us is susceptible to the ravages of disease or the result of some terrible accident. That's life. Sparrows do fall! How you deal with it is more important than the answer to those entire "Why?" questions.

During many weeks of recuperation while I was out of the pulpit, I struggled with the decision of resigning as pastor of the church. That decision was as difficult as the decision to become a pastor in the first place thirty years previously.

The first day I became pastor of that church I walked into the pastor's study, knelt down by my desk and prayed that God would tell me when it was time to resign. During my recovery from surgery the conviction that I should resign became stronger. I prayed that if God wanted me to resign that he would send a pulpit committee from another church to invite me to be their pastor. This He did not do. After praying for many months for a pulpit committee to come and none came, the Holy Spirit assured me it was time to resign anyway. This I did.

The following year was very difficult as I tried to reconcile my call to preach with the fact that no opportunities presented themselves for me to do so. This I could not understand. My sense of frustration intensified until finally the Holy Spirit gave me the promise recorded in Jeremiah 29:11 (LB) "I know the plans I have for you, says the Lord. They are plans for good and not for evil, to give you a future and a hope." I knew then that whatever God had planned for me was for my good, whether I could understand it or not. The ensuing years have verified this truth far beyond my expectations!

Sometimes, when sparrows fall, we simply have to trust the Lord without an answer to the question, "Why?"

CHAPTER FIVE

A Terminal Illness

The birth of a grandchild is always an exciting time, but when it is overshadowed by diagnostic surgery which reveals the baby has a terminal illness, that excitement immediately turns to heart-wrenching pain.

Abby, our first granddaughter was born the day after Christmas in 1980. She was a beautiful baby, a belated Christmas gift from God, a source of joy. She looked so precious lying there in her crib at the hospital, so much so, that I called her "Precious" that first day and many times thereafter. But as we stood there watching the nurses hovering over Abby I said to Anna, "Something is wrong with our baby." The way the nurses were working with her indicated to me that something was not as it should be.

Suspecting something very serious, in the middle of the night they took her by helicopter (Med Flight) to University Children's Hospital in Oklahoma City (coincidentally the same hospital I was in when I had polio twenty-eight years before) where the doctors performed abdominal surgery and found a blockage in her small intestine. They removed the obstruction which they referred to as a "meconium ileus" and performed a colostomy. Abby's pediatrician who was originally from Yugoslavia sat with us during the surgery. She told us many children in her country had this type of surgery, but she did not fully reveal to us the implications or possibilities.

The next day when Lou and Anna were with Abby, a new doctor, Dr. Flux, came in to examine her. He casually referred to the disease, cystic fibrosis (we had already been informed of this "possibility" and its implications) and Anna said, "I know you can't be definite but approximately what percentage of these children turn out to have this disease?" He said, "You mean no one has informed you of this?" She said, "No, we were only told they would run some tests." He was visibly angry and said, "They should have told you immediately! There is no need for testing. Her type of surgery is in and of itself diagnostic of Cystic Fibrosis." He left the room as they stood there trying to absorb the full impact of what he had just told them. He returned shortly thereafter and said, "I am so sorry about this. This is the damndest disease I have ever encountered. They are always talking about a cure but it will not happen in my lifetime and certainly not in hers. I will set up an appointment for someone to meet and explain this to you." We later met with a lady doctor who told us, "This disease is incurable and it is terminal. Some children live a year or two and some live to be five or six. With her involvement she may live two years. These children are usually very bright and very happy so take her home and enjoy her."

Cystic Fibrosis causes excessive mucus formation throughout the body. It attacks the digestive system and prevents the person from receiving nourishment from the food they eat. It also affects their pancreas and lungs, and the air sacks begin to fill with mucus which must be dislodged as much as possible. This is done by cupping the hand and beating on their chest and back for twenty to thirty minutes two or three times daily, and then having them cough hard to bring up the mucus and spit it out. After a period of years their lungs become so scarred there is no room left for air, and what room is left is filled with mucus and they die from frequent bouts of pneumonia and lack of oxygen.

A darker, more hopeless, despairing picture could not have been painted. It was as though the doctor had painted a picture of her condition and entitled it, "No Hope".

How do you deal with such awful and dreadful news? What do you say to your daughter whose joy of motherhood has just been broken and shattered? What do you say to your wife whose dreams as a grandmother have been distorted by such dreadful news? What do you say to your loved ones and friends who seem so helpless when they hear the doctor's report? Moreover, what do you say to God? Do you say, "That's okay, Lord, we can handle it" as the tears leave your eyes, roll down your cheeks, and drop to the floor? Then later, when there is no one around to hear and see, you weep and wail loudly, no longer able to contain your emotions when you are free to express your sorrow.

So, after the initial weeping and wailing were over, with what little faith remained we began a prayer vigil which was to last for thirteen years and finally end seemingly without an answer from God. We prayed for her healing to the very end until she was in such pain we finally prayed for her deliverance from that body of death. What do you do when God does not answer your prayers? What do you do when God "disappoints" you? Do you give up on God? Do you stop praying altogether? Do you turn your back on God because He did not do what you asked him to do; or do you draw closer to him to find strength to help in time of need? The choice was ours. The choice is yours.

Dare we be honest enough to blame God for not doing what we asked him to? Dare we challenge him? Call him to account? Or do we simply acquiesce to his will? Are we bold enough and comfortable enough in our faith to confront the Lord with his inaction as were Mary and Martha? (John 11:1-45) "Lord, it's your fault our brother died. If you had come when we asked you to he would not have died." Mary and Martha voice what most of us are afraid or hesitant to voice—

accusation, blame, fault, censure, reprimand, and question. Yet Jesus understands their emotions and does not rebuke, but rather comforts them with his personal promise and gentle reminder that he himself is the resurrection and the life. Neither will he rebuke us for being honest with him about our feelings and our faith or lack thereof.

She was a beautiful, bright, happy child and we were blessed to have her with us for those thirteen years even though our hearts ached and hurt because every day she lived she fought for each breath she took. I suffered many things along life's road, including Polio, the death of my parents in a car wreck, the dying and death of three brothers and two sisters and their spouses, my wife's fight with cancer, the death of Anna's parents, and other situations not referenced in these essays, but nothing comparable to what Abby endured. I accepted all of these without question, not without sorrow, but without question. However, this, the suffering of my granddaughter brought me to despair. It tried my faith more than all the others put together. Like Job, I thought God owed me an explanation.

A typical day for Abby was one that raised many questions in our mind. Would God just please explain to me why Abby had to greet each day with a handful of pills and "clapping" exercises on her chest and back to relieve, as much as possible, the congestion and cough and then have to repeat those two or three times during the day! Would He help me understand why on many occasions she had to have three continuous weeks of intravenous treatments when her little veins were too small for the needles! And why did she have to have a feeding tube every night (which she had learned to put in by herself when she was only five years old) in order to get the nourishment she needed!

Abby dealt with this disease better than the rest of us. She accepted her condition and never complained as far as I know. She never gave in to it; she fought it with every ounce of energy she had. Her faith, courage, and spirit were contagious. Her sense of humor provided many moments of laughter. In spite of the disease she was Abby (our source of joy). Her intelligence was far beyond her years and overwhelmed us. She remained on the Honor Roll even during her last weeks she attended school. Her beautiful singing made us proud and blessed the lives of many, many people as she sang solos at her church and also in the Crystal Cathedral in California.

As the final days of her life upon this earth approached she grew weaker and weaker and trips to the hospital for treatments occurred more frequently. Abby loved to read during her lifetime and spent many pleasurable hours with her books. During her final extended stay in the hospital, her Uncle Jeff, who was also her school principal, would come after school and sit by her bedside and spend hours reading to her. She and her Uncle Jeff were kindred spirits, they were both avid readers, and when he came and read to her those were some of her brightest hours.

Her final trip to the hospital and her last days were filled with apprehension for all of us; however she dealt with the dying process and her approaching death with the same spirit and faith which she had exercised all of her life. The only time I ever heard of her complaining was a few hours before she died she did say to her grandmother, "My life hurts." There is a book entitled, TRUSTING GOD EVEN WHEN LIFE HURTS. That is exactly what Abby did!

The final hour for her departure arrived and Abby requested all the family to come so she could tell each of them good-bye. One by one we leaned over her bed and said our farewells.

Abby finally became so weak that she told her mother she wanted to go ahead and die and to remove the machines and oxygen. Her mother, Lou, did so and held her in her arms. Apparently Abby thought she would die immediately and when she didn't she asked her mother, "Why does it take so long to die?"

The doctor came in and informed us that the dying process would be so much easier for Abby if we would replace the oxygen, which would enable her to breathe without difficulty while her body produced a natural anesthetic. The oxygen was replaced.

Lou had told Abby that when the time came she would sing her into Heaven. So Lou lay on the bed with her, cradled her in her arms and began to sing and continued singing as Abby left her earthly body and entered her Heavenly home.

There was a brief family graveside service for Abby and later a memorial service in which she was honored for her faith, spirit, friendliness, encouragement, joy, and all the lives she had touched in her thirteen years upon this earth. She was a good steward of her suffering and a challenge to others to also be good stewards of their sufferings.

How you respond when sparrows fall is far more important than trying to find the answer to the question, "Why?" Yet we keep asking the question and keep searching for the answer, and that is acceptable because that is one of the ways we work through suffering and tragedy, disease and death.

The passing of time gives a new perspective of the issues of life, especially the fall of sparrows. A few months prior to the first year anniversary of Abby's death, which occurred on May 18, 1994, Anna and I were sitting in the family room and she said, "You need to write a memorial about Abby so we can put it in the paper on the anniversary date of her death." Although our hearts have ached and many tears have fallen, many precious memories have brought joy and laughter even in the midst of our sorrow just as Abby did from the day she was born. Her name means "Source of Joy" which she truly was and is. I wrote the following from the perspective of one who believes that Jesus Christ is who the Bible says he is and that his promises are true.

REMEMBERING YOU—ABBY
OUR SOURCE OF JOY
She is God's own personal possession.
No longer in our hands, but His.
She lives in His presence in Heaven,

No longer with us, but with Him.

Although saddened by her absence,
We are lifted by her life.
The joy which she provided,
Overcomes our sorrow and strife.

Trapped in a cystic fibrosis body at birth,
She fought for every breath she took.
But she never complained and never frowned,
She simply smiled and kidded around.

Her faith, her smile, her laugh, her wit
Was a blessing beyond compare.
And the life she lived and the lives she touched,
Will forever be
Our Source of Joy, ABBY.

Abby was fond of rainbows. On the day when her mother, Lou Ann, decided it was time to "let go" and rejoice in Abby's life, we all gathered together at her graveside and released balloons as a symbol of releasing Abby from this life and acknowledging her new life in Heaven. On a beautiful clear sunny day as we released those balloons and watched them rise into the sky we saw a magnificent rainbow directly over our heads! It was as if Abby were smiling and approving our actions.

There were other significant rainbows and birds. Both Abby's mother and Aunt Kendra had similar experiences:

In His Time

"My niece, Abby, was diagnosed with cystic fibrosis at birth. When she was a baby, I had a memorable time of prayer when I earnestly prayed, in faith believing, God would heal her. I asked God for a sign. There was a bird singing outside my window during this time of prayer. I specifically prayed that if He was going to heal her, would he please send the bird to land on the window sill, so, I would know that it was in His plans to heal her. The bird never landed.

When Abby was thirteen years old she died. Grief was heavy as we left the hospital after her death. I arrived home around 1:00-1:30 a.m. When I got out of my car to head into my home, a bird was loudly singing and I instantly knew it was God saying "I have healed her!" There was no question in my heart that God had given me the sign I had asked for so many years ago. His plan and mine were different but He heard, He answered, and He healed her.

The next day, I shared with my sister, Abby's mom, about my prayer many years ago asking God to heal Abby and how God had answered the night of Abby's death with the sign of the singing bird. My sister began to share with me her story----":

"It was the night of May 18th, 1994. The sky was so clear and the stars were shining so brightly, filling up the night sky. The air was calm and crisp. It was all so very peaceful and quiet, nothing like the turmoil and grief going on inside my heart, soul, and mind. You see, I had just arrived home after having left the hospital where my 13-year-old daughter, Abby, who was born with cystic fibrosis, had passed away at 10:30 p.m.

It was now about 2:00 a.m. and I was at home sitting on the front porch with my youngest daughter Hanna. You might ask why were we sitting there at that time, and not going inside our home? I now know that God planned it that way. At the time, I really didn't even think about why other than I didn't have my house key and so my parents went to get one. They wanted us to go with them but I just wanted to sit on the porch with Hanna. As we sat and waited, it was so quiet and calm. We cried a little and held on to each other and sat quietly.

I remember thinking I didn't want to go into the house without Abby. How would I be able to do that? I had such an enormously empty feeling. Yet, I had Hanna sitting beside me, arm in arm, offering me a quiet comfort.

Although our grief felt like more than we could bear, we also had a knowledge and assurance that Abby was in Heaven with Jesus. I was also thinking about how she was no longer in pain and could sing and laugh without coughing or running out of breath. You see, Abby loved to sing songs of praise and worship to Christ. In the midst of living with cystic fibrosis, singing brought a comfort, peace, and joy to her soul. Even though she was always short of breath, Abby didn't allow the disease to rob her of the joy of singing. Enough so, that she wanted to leave this world and enter Heaven singing praises. Abby and I had an understanding that when it was evident she was near her end here on earth, that she and I would sing her to Heaven. So on this night, although she had been unconscious for several hours, Abby was aware enough to speak one word, "mom". I knew then it was time to sing. So I got into her bed, held her in my arms, and began singing praises and hymns. Abby was unable to sing with her mouth but I know within her heart and soul she was singing as God called her home. How do I know? Because, as I found out later, her oxygen levels increased while we were singing, but more important than that, Abby knew it was time to meet her Heavenly Father and she was ready to sing before Him.

So, as I sat on the porch with Hanna in the stillness of the night, God gave us the joy of hearing Abby sing one more time. No, she wasn't singing in her human voice, but through the singing of one solitary bird. I say singing because the song from the bird was not just a bunch of whistles or chirps but it was one long continuous melody. Hanna and I just looked at each other and said, "It's Abby". We knew it was God's way of letting us know she was with Him. We laughed and cried at the joy and peace of knowing Abby was with God and singing in full breath to Him. With a calm assurance that only God can give, we quietly listened to the singing of praises and thanksgiving offered by our song bird Abby."

Along with Kendra's and Lou's experiences with rainbows and birds, on several of my visits to her graveside during the next two or three years either rainbows or birds would appear. One special event occurred as I sat by her grave. A small bird came and perched on a limb of a Bradford Pear tree at the head of her grave. As Abby loved to sing, it began to sing and hop from branch to branch. After a few moments it flew away as if to say, "OK, Granddad, that's enough!"

As a result of those very personal and blessed experiences with rainbows and birds, I wrote the following in an effort to express what they mean to me:

OF RAINBOWS AND BIRDS

Through rainbows and birds she spoke to me,
As I stood by her graveside beneath the tree.
She smiled through the rainbows and sang through the birds
And as I listened, this is what I heard:

She spoke of freedom and blessings and joy untold.
She spoke of love and beauty and joy to behold.

She spoke of fullness and wholeness and joy abounding.
She spoke of breath and health and joy surrounding.

She spoke of life and light and joy for all.
She spoke of peace and comfort and joy to all.

Through rainbows and birds she spoke to me,
As I stood by her graveside beneath the tree.

In spite of the sorrow, the heartache, the sense of loss and the physical separation there is still hope when a sparrow falls. The Word of God speaks of this hope: Romans 15:13 "Now the God of <u>hope</u> fill you with all joy and peace in believing, that ye may abound in <u>hope</u>, through the power of the Holy Ghost."— Titus 1:2 "In <u>hope</u> of eternal life, which God, that cannot lie, promised before the world began."— Titus 2:13 "Looking for that blessed <u>hope</u>, and the glorious appearing of the great God and our Saviour Jesus Christ."—Titus 3:7 "That being justified by his grace, we should be made heirs according to the <u>hope</u> of eternal life."—Hebrews 6:19 "Which <u>hope</u> we have as an anchor of the soul, both sure and steadfast"—I Peter 1:3 "Blessed be the God and Father of our Lord Jesus Christ, which according to his abundant mercy hath begotten us again unto a lively <u>hope</u> by the resurrection of Jesus Christ from the dead."

Consider the very personal experience of Mary and Martha recorded in the eleventh chapter of the Gospel According to John: In essence they said, "Lord, it's your fault he died!" Dare we be honest enough to blame God for not doing what we asked him to do? "If you had come when we asked you to things would have turned out better!" Is that true? Which would have been better, really? The healing of Lazarus or bringing him back to life after he had died and had been dead for four days! By allowing Lazarus to die and, after four days, raising him from the dead Jesus demonstrated his power over death and proved that he, himself, was indeed the resurrection and the life!

Jesus let nature take its course and Lazarus died. But afterward, Jesus undid what nature had done! He reversed the experience of death; he overcame death; he acted beyond death to give hope of life beyond physical death! Do you have such a hope as this? If not, consider Jesus. He died on the cross for the sins of all, rose from the dead on the third day, and said, "I am the resurrection and the life and because I live you shall live also.

Martha voices what most of us are afraid or hesitant to voice— accusations, blame, fault. Yet Jesus understands her emotions and does not rebuke her, but rather comforts her with his personal pronouncement and gentle reminder that He himself is the resurrection and the life! He ministers to our broken heart and shattered faith. Slowly he replaces the anxiety, stress, and panic with his peace, joy, and the sense of safety normally found in our faith.

To be sure Jesus did not respond to her plea in a timely manner as far as she was concerned; however, it was timely for his purpose! "If you had been here my brother would not have died; but I know even now that God will do whatever you ask." Her faith in his power was not diminished, but her disappointment in his untimely response was evident. Who of us cannot relate to this? Have we not all experienced the fall of a sparrow, a spouse, a child, a grandchild, a friend, a loved one taken away from us by death or an unrelenting illness destroying their health, and we hoped and prayed for healing, but healing never came and nature took its course? We are devastated, our faith is challenged, and we cry "Unfair" to God, screaming in our soul, "God, do something!"?

Consider this: No man can tell God what to do, not even through prayer. The purpose of prayer is not to command God. You cannot command God. Give up the idea that you can control God. You can tell him what you would like for him to do but you cannot command him to do it. In fact we are encouraged "to let your requests be made known unto God" and thereby obtain the peace of God which keeps our hearts and minds through Christ Jesus (Philippians 4:6-7); but there are no guarantees.

Many books have been written on prayer with the theme of "asking and receiving". Some of those books deal with "formulas" and "techniques" for getting God to do something for you or give you something. If you rely on those teachings, sooner or later you will be disappointed. There are no prayer "formulas" or prayer "techniques" that guarantee God will act like you want him to act. The best way to approach prayer is to present your requests to God remembering that he is your Heavenly Father who loves you and always wants what is best for you. Trust him!

No man can make God go any direction they choose. Many have tried and failed; therefore many have rejected the God of the Bible. They want a god they can control, a god who will do their bidding and allow them to do whatever they please. They want a god who will not interfere with their lifestyle. The God of the Bible does not fit their criteria morally, mentally, or socially. They want a god who is intellectually acceptable to them and their peers, a "fashionable" god, a "politically correct" god, and a god who does not require a moral standard. Therefore they fabricate a god; they design a god of their own choosing and reject the God of the Bible, the God who made them. (Romans 1:21-32) If we would have the God of the Bible we must accept him as he is revealed in the Bible.

According to the Bible there is only one true and living God. When it comes to defining God our definition must begin and end with the Bible. Once we step outside the Bible for a definition of God, that opens the door to all kinds of lesser gods, gods of man's own making, gods of man's imagination, gods made in the image of man rather than the God who made man in His image!

God is not always going to do what we ask or act like we think he should, so when God "disappoints" us in this manner we must trust Him, His wisdom, His love and His purpose. After all, who wants to worship a god made by some man? But to worship the God who created man is something else! God does not dance to our tune nor does he take turns playing "Mother May I" or move in response to "Simon Says". Who wants to worship a god they can manipulate! Who wants to worship a puppet made by some man!

There are no "prayer guarantees". There are prayer promises but no guarantees that God will give us what we ask for or that God will do what we ask Him to do. No man can take the prayer promises and use them to manipulate God. Our understanding of the prayer promises must allow God to remain in charge at all times. At no point will God ever abdicate His throne to any man, prayer promises or no prayer promises. There are no prayer promises which place man in charge instead of God—no health guarantees, no wealth guarantees, no guarantees from rape, murder, robbery, disease, death, fire, flood or any of the other ravages of nature or man.

Our granddaughter, Abby, lived with Cystic Fibrosis for thirteen years fighting for every breath she took, forcing herself to the limit to be as active as possible, suffering the pain and enduring the limitations of CF and finally dying. Having observed her struggle for those thirteen years we had questions that challenged the very foundation of our faith. Did we not pray? Did we not fast? Did we not ask and ask and ask? Did we not agree on what to ask? Did we not claim all the prayer promises? Why then did God not answer our prayers for her healing? Yes, there is some comfort in knowing that God knows when the sparrow falls; but the question is "Why doesn't He do something about it?"

Where is Jesus while all of this is going on? He is on His way with a greater miracle than mere healing. He is on His way with the miracle of life, the miracle of resurrection! A greater good is involved here than mere healing, the glory of God is in this experience! We must remember that when life is at its worst God is at His best! Witness Jesus before the boy with the demon, saying, "Come out of him!" Witness Jesus at the tomb of Lazarus, "Lazarus, come forth!" Witness Jesus on the cross, saying, "Today shalt thou be with me in paradise!" Witness God's promise after my parents' funeral, "Fear thou not for I am with thee; be not dismayed for I am thy God. I will strengthen thee, yea, I will help thee, yea, I will uphold thee with the right hand of my righteousness!"

A personal question: Even though you send word (through prayer) to Jesus that your loved one is sick (as did Mary and Martha) but He does not come to heal your loved one and your loved one dies (as did Lazarus) will you still trust Him and find comfort and hope in the reality that Jesus himself defeated death? In John 14:19 Jesus said, "Because I live, ye shall live also." In light of his death, burial, and resurrection we believe that we and our loved ones also shall continue to live with Him beyond this earthly life. That is our hope, and such a hope provides an exceedingly great comfort when sparrows fall. II Corinthians 4:8, 9, 14, 16 and 5:1, 6-8, expresses our hope: "----We are troubled on every side, yet not distressed; we are perplexed, but not in despair; persecuted, but not forsaken; cast down, but not destroyed----knowing that he which raised up the Lord Jesus shall raise up us also by Jesus, and shall present us with you. ----For which cause we faint not; but though our outward man perish, yet the inward man is renewed day by day. For our light affliction, which is but for a moment, worketh for us a far more exceeding and eternal weight of glory; while we look not at the things which are seen, but at the things which are not seen: for the things which are seen are temporal; but the things which are not seen are eternal. For we know that if our earthly house of this tabernacle were dissolved, we have a building of God, an house not made with hands, eternal in the heavens.----Therefore we are always confident, knowing that, while we are at home in the body, we are absent from the Lord: (For we walk by faith, not by sight:) We are confident, I say, and willing rather to be absent from the body, and to be present with the Lord."

There are lessons to learn, sorrows to endure, heartaches to embrace, tears to shed, wounds to heal, faith to exercise and life to live when sparrows fall! There's a blessing in the burden!

"What a Friend we have in Jesus, all our sins and griefs to bear!
What a privilege to carry everything to God in prayer!
O what peace we often forfeit, O what needless pain we bear,
All because we do not carry everything to God in prayer!

Have we trials and temptations! Is there trouble anywhere?
We should never be discouraged, take it to the Lord in prayer.
Can we find a friend so faithful Who will all our sorrows share?
Jesus knows our every weakness, take it to the Lord in prayer.

Are we weak and heavy laden, cumbered with a load of care?
Precious Saviour, still our refuge, take it to the Lord in prayer.
Do thy friends despise, forsake thee? Take it to the Lord in prayer;
In His arms He'll take and shield thee, thou wilt find a solace there."
Words: Joseph Scriven, 1855 Music: Charles C. Converse, 1868

CHAPTER SIX

A Sparrow Falls at Calvary

The ultimate sparrow to fall, which affected my life more than any other, was God's own Son! As the blood of that first sparrow, which fell in my life that day back in 1938, spread across the snow, so the blood of God's own Sparrow which fell at Calvary the day Christ was crucified, spread across my sin-darkened heart and washed it white as snow.

Consider the fall of that heavenly Sparrow and perhaps you will discover the solution to all suffering and the answer to the question, "Why?" Consider the suffering of the most noble Sparrow of all and what God has accomplished through that suffering, and ask yourself the question: "Can it be that all the blessings that come from the fall of sparrows far out-weigh the heartaches and suffering associated with it?" Jesus certainly thought so according to Isaiah 53:11 "He shall see of the travail of his soul, and shall be satisfied..."

When he considered the suffering of his soul and compared it to what the results would be, the Suffering Servant was satisfied. Surely when we shall see the travail of our souls from Heaven's perspective, we also shall be satisfied. Most assuredly, we shall be satisfied with the results of our suffering when we see them in Heaven. Did Paul not write in Romans 8:18, "For I reckon that the sufferings of this present time are not worthy to be compared with the glory which shall be revealed in us."? Hebrews 12:1-3 indicates the same wonderful truth: "...let us run with patience the race that is set before us, looking unto Jesus the author and finisher of our faith; who for the joy that was set before him endured the cross, despising the shame, and is set down at the right hand of the throne of God." Without a doubt the blessings shall by far outweigh the sufferings! There's a blessing in the burden!

Consider the fall of that divine Sparrow and what God did with and through all of the sorrow, tragedy, injustice, pain and suffering which He endured. As the blood of my first sparrow to fall spread across the snow, so the blood of Jesus Christ continues to spread across the world changing lives and blessing humanity. Is it too much to think that if that much good came out of that much suffering, surely God can bless others through our suffering? The blessings which come from the fall of sparrows far surpass the heartaches. "And we know that in all things God works for the good of those who love him, who have been called according to his purpose."(Romans 8:28 NIV) This truth only comes through faith in the love, sovereignty, power, and purposes of Almighty God. There is a blessing in the burden, look for it. "My brethren, count it all joy, consider yourselves happy indeed, when various trials come upon you, knowing this, that the trial of your faith works patience and develops endurance; but let patience do a thorough job that you may be fully developed and perfectly equipped lacking in nothing"(James 1:2-4)

As we consider the fall of the ultimate Sparrow I would like to consider his humanity first and then, when we come to his ultimate suffering, consider his Divinity.

Acknowledging the fact that Jesus Christ was and is the one and only begotten Son of God and that He was and is God incarnate (God in flesh), virgin born and sinless, let's look at the fall of this Sparrow primarily from the standpoint of His humanity. He was, after all, a common man, this carpenter from Nazareth. He quite often referred to Himself as "the son of man". That term, referring to Jesus, appears eighty-five times in the New Testament—81 times in the Four Gospels (Mathew, Mark, Luke, and John), and 4 times in Acts, Hebrews, and Revelation.

As far as men go Jesus was a common man. His birth was common. His childhood was common. His teen years were common. His occupation was common. The entire earthly life of Jesus was common up to the point where His Divinity (Godness) could no longer be hidden. At that point, like a light dispelling darkness, His oneness with God shone through, revealing itself in the midst of His humanity. Otherwise, although He was God in a human body, Jesus was a common man.

- Consider his birth: nothing auspicious about that. In fact, the circumstances surrounding his birth reflect a commonality which places him slightly below the common man. He was born in Bethlehem as the result of a Royal decree requiring every citizen to register for taxation in the city of his linage. Consequently, Mary, who was pregnant with Jesus, went with Joseph, her fiancé, from Nazareth to Bethlehem to register for that taxation. When they arrived, due to the excessive number of people required to register in Bethlehem, there was no room available for them in the local inn. Since Mary's time to give birth was imminent, they received permission to stay in a stable with the cattle and sheep. That night she gave birth to her firstborn, wrapped him in birthing clothes, and laid him in a manger filled with hay for the animals. Nothing auspicious about that!

- Consider his childhood: Nothing outstanding or exceptional about that either. Other than his presentation at the Temple and his flight to Egypt to escape Herod's wrath, only his trip to Jerusalem when he was twelve years old is recorded in the Bible. There was nothing outstanding about that event either, except his interaction with the Scribes, because a visit to the Temple at the age of twelve was a common Jewish tradition.

- Consider his teenage years: The rest of his childhood and teen years are summed up in two verses in Luke 2:51-52: "He went down with them, and came to Nazareth, and was subject unto them; and Jesus increased in wisdom and stature and in favor with God and man." That's what any teenage Jewish boy should have done, nothing unusual about that.

- Consider his adult life: His was a common vocation. He was a carpenter. At one point they derisively said of him, "'Is not this the carpenter, the son of Mary?', and they were offended at him." (Mark 6:3) "The carpenter": a common vocation.

From all outward appearances Jesus was an ordinary, run of the mill man, who, when he was hungry he ate; when he was thirsty he drank; when he was tired he rested; when he was wounded he bled; when he was sad he cried. He had no credentials, no royal decree recognizing him as a prince or king, no religious scroll authorizing him to speak or teach or preach in the Temple. Matthew 21:23 tells about the chief priests and elders saying to Jesus, "By what authority do you do these things? Who gave you this authority? Where are your credentials?" He was a common man with no social or religious standing. He was far from being affluent. He had no place to lay his head and when he needed money to pay taxes he had to find it in the mouth of a fish, and when he died his body was laid in a borrowed tomb. As a man Jesus owned no earthly property except the clothes on his back. (However, as Creator-God he owned everything!)

Even when it came to his physical appearance, Jesus had nothing special going for him in that department either. There was nothing unusual about his countenance, nothing outstanding or attractive about his physical appearance. "For he shall grow up before him as a tender plant, and as a root out of a dry ground: he hath no form nor comeliness; and when we shall see him, there is no beauty that we should desire him." (Isaiah 53:2)

There was nothing about his physical appearance that would indicate who he was. When Jesus asked the question, "Who do men say that I the Son of man am?" Peter replied, "You are the Christ, the Son of the living God." Then Jesus said, "Flesh and blood (physical appearance or human intellect) has not revealed this to you but my Father who is in heaven." In other words, Peter could not tell who Jesus was just by looking at him, nor could he deduce by human reasoning who Jesus was. The Father through the ministry of the Holy Spirit revealed Jesus' Divinity to Peter. There was nothing remarkable or extraordinary about his physical appearance that would attract people to him. Yet there was something about what he said and what he did that, like a magnet, drew people to him. They said of him, "Never man spoke like this man; we have never seen it on this fashion; he did all things well."

When Jesus was thirty-years-old he became an itinerant teacher-preacher traversing the land of Palestine, back and forth across Judea, Samaria, and Galilee; however, he was never recognized nor accepted by the religious leaders of his day. In fact, they laughed at him, resented him, ridiculed him, resisted him, rejected him, and ultimately crucified him. Remember in Mark 6:2-3 even the fickle crowd was bragging on him one minute, "What a wonderful speaker He is. He does all things well." but the next thing you know they are denigrating him and belittling him saying, "He's only a carpenter! He doesn't have any real credentials. Why his brothers and sisters live right here in town. He himself grew up here. He's nobody special." Even his own brothers did not see him other than as a delusional person who needed help. "And when his friends heard of it, they went to lay hold on him: for they said, He is beside himself (Mark 3:21). "For neither did his brethren believe in him." (John 7:5). Even his followers, the apostles, did not grasp the full meaning of his teaching concerning his death and resurrection. At this point many of them could not see beyond his humanity. When the time came for him to be arrested and sentenced to die by crucifixion, one openly denied him and the others deserted him and locked themselves behind closed doors for fear of also being arrested and executed.

Now that we have looked at the fall of the ultimate Sparrow from the standpoint of his humanity, we must go beyond his humanity to his Divinity (Godness) to capture the total significance of his suffering and death, because if Jesus was a man and only a man then his fall (death) is of no more significance than the fall (death) of any other sparrow. But if he was who he said he was, the only begotten Son of God, one with the Father himself, God in the flesh, then his fall takes on majestic and Divine proportions, and impacts humanity beyond description.

He was more than a human being. He was Divine. He was the God-Being. He was God! Declarations of his Divinity are apparent in the prophesies concerning him and in the accounts of his conception, birth, presentation in the Temple, teachings, activities, death, burial, resurrection, and ascension. His Divinity was also declared by Simeon, Anna, Jesus himself, John the Baptist, Peter, Thomas, one of the soldiers assisting with his crucifixion, and the Apostle Paul in his writings.

At the point of his suffering, we must go beyond his humanity, because the suffering he did in the flesh was nothing compared to the suffering he endured in his soul, as God's Holy and Righteous Son, as the sins of all people for all time were placed upon him. Our sins and our iniquities which were placed upon him were heavier than the cross he bore, sharper than the nails which pierced his hands and feet, more painful than the spear thrust into his side, more stinging than the crown of thorns pressed into his brow, and more torturous than the lacerations across his back. No physical suffering can compare to the suffering which the Holy Son of God endured during this ignominious death as the sins of the world were placed upon his sinless soul. The ultimate pain and suffering, which Jesus endured while dying on the cross for our sins, can be heard and felt in that unfathomable cry, "My God, my God, why hast thou forsaken me?"

Considering the "Why?" of the suffering and death of Jesus Christ, should we bring God into the center of this picture? If not, let's be realistic, and see this picture without God. Without God, if Jesus was just a man and nothing but a man, then all we see is the animosity of religious men calling for the crucifixion of a fellow Jew, the authorization of that crucifixion by Pilate, the performance of their duties by the soldiers who drove those nails through his hands and his feet, lifting the cross into its upright position, piercing his side with a spear, and leaving him hanging there to die. The result: one dead Jew. If God is not in this picture Jesus is just another dead man, one among many.

However, we must add God to this picture because God placed himself in this picture and brought himself into this "fallen" world when Jesus was born to Mary in Bethlehem. "And she shall bring forth a son, and thou shalt call his name JESUS: for he shall save his people from their sins. Now all this was done, that it might be fulfilled which was spoken of the Lord by the prophet, saying, "Behold, a virgin shall be with child, and shall bring forth a son, and they shall call his name Emmanuel, which being interpreted is, God with us." (Matthew 1:21-23; Isaiah 7:14). Also "—God was in Christ, reconciling the world unto himself." (II Corinthians 5:19) Jesus made it very clear that God is in this world picture when he answered Philip's request to "show us the Father": "Have I been so long time with you, and yet hast thou not known me, Philip? he that hath seen me hath seen the Father; how sayest thou then, Show us the Father? Believest thou not that I am in the Father, and the Father in me? the words that I speak unto you I speak not of myself: but the Father that dwelleth in me, he doeth the works." (John 14:9-10)

Herein, in the fall of this Sparrow, the greatest Sparrow of all, we find the answer to the question, "Why?" which comes with the fall of all sparrows. Even the Son of God himself asked the "Why?" question: "My God, My God <u>why</u> hast thou forsaken me?" True, the Father did not answer his only begotten Son and he may not answer us, but the answer lies in the suffering of the greatest Sparrow ever to fall. That Sparrow suffered more than all other sparrows combined!

Please seriously consider the following truths which reveal the extent of the pain He endured:

- The weight of our sins was heavier than the cross he carried.
- When our sins were placed upon his sinless soul he suffered more than when the nails were driven through his hands and feet.
- It was not the nails that held him there; it was his love for us and his Father's will.
- The mocking and scoffing of the crowd stung him more than the thorns on his brow.
- The unbelief and betrayal by Judas, his friend, cut deeper than the lashes on his back.
- The denial by Peter pierced his heart more than the spear that pierced his side.
- The desertion by his disciples was more humiliating than the plucking of his beard and the spitting in his face.
- Being forsaken by the Father was more excruciating than all the physical pain he endured!

As Jesus faced this horrible event of taking upon himself the sins of the world, he went to his favorite place of prayer in the Garden of Gethsemane. Due to the struggle he was facing he left his disciples at the edge, and went farther into the trees to commune with the Father in private. He knelt in prayer and as he faced this horrifying ordeal of his soul, he was in such agony that he sweat, as it were, great drops of blood. (Luke 22:44) He dreaded being made sin so much he asked his Father if there was any way to escape having to drink this cup of suffering.

You may be able to understand, to some degree, the soul-suffering of Jesus if you realize that the sins of all mankind, from Adam to the last person who will ever be born, were placed upon him, the Holy sinless Son of God! Then think of the most despicable, horrid, revolting, repugnant, degrading, sordid, and vile sin you can imagine and how "dirty" it makes you feel just thinking of it. Multiply that awful feeling by infinity and you have a slight understanding of how "dirty and degraded and horrible" Jesus must have felt when the actual sins of all men of all time were laid on him. After all, if some sins make us sinners feel "dirty and degraded", how much more the sinless Son of God!

Surely He cringed at the very thought of becoming sin. How tortuous it must have been for the sinless Son of God when all our loathsome and odious sins were placed on him at Calvary. Think of it, the sinless One being inundated with sin, the sins of the world, the very antithesis of his sinless nature. That is exactly what occurred on the cross! "For he hath made him to be sin for us, who knew no sin; that we might be made the righteousness of God in him." (II Corinthians 5:21) He entered the bottomless pit of suffering for us. Oh the horror of the sinless Son of God being made sin!

Let us briefly review the suffering of Jesus: misunderstanding, rejection, betrayal, abandonment, verbal abuse, denial, loss of friends, mockery, the maltreatment of his physical features by the crushing of the crown of thorns upon his brow, the jerking out of his beard, the lashing and beating of his back, the marring of his visage more than any man's, so much so, the people were appalled at his appearance, his body disfigured by the entire crucifixion episode, and finally that unforgettable cry from the cross, "My God, my God, why hast thou forsaken me?". That haunting cry was the culmination of the physical body and spiritual soul suffering endured by our Savior, to say nothing of the pain of the Father!

The Son was not the only one who was suffering that day; the Father and the Holy Spirit were also suffering!

In Ephesians 4:28-31 Paul provides a list of sins which grieve the Holy Spirit. Imagine those sins being cast upon Jesus and consider how sad the Holy Spirit must have been. If those sins in our life cause the Holy Spirit to sorrow and grieve, how much more grief and suffering was inflicted upon the Holy Spirit when the Holy Son of God was made to be sin! Extend that grief and suffering to the Nth degree and you get some semblance of the suffering, sorrow, and grief experienced by the Godhead (Father, Son, and Holy Spirit).

Now consider the pain of the Father. But first consider your pain as you see your own child suffering and your hurt is so deep you hide your head in your hands and cry uncontrollably. As a father or mother you know what you experience when your children suffer. When they suffer you suffer. When they cry you cry. When they hurt you hurt. When they mourn you mourn. When they groan under a burden you groan. How much more the Heavenly Father for his only Son! Can you fathom the pain of the Father as he had to turn his back on his only Son in the very midst of his suffering? At the very height of Jesus' suffering, when he was made sin for us, the Father had to turn his back on his only Son and let him suffer and die alone! Oh, how that cry from the cross (My God, my God, why hast thou forsaken me?) must have wrenched the heart of the Father! Surely the suffering of the Son, to say nothing of the pain of the Father and the Holy Spirit, tells us how much God loves us!

Who would ever have thought that God's love, forgiveness, mercy, and saving grace would be so inextricably intertwined with such suffering! Yet, in Isaiah, Chapter 53 (NIV) this very truth is magnified by his prophesies of the suffering Servant (Christ): "He had no beauty or majesty to attract us to him, nothing in his appearance that we should desire him. He was despised and rejected by men, a man of sorrows, and familiar with suffering. Like one from whom men hide their faces he was despised, and we esteemed him not. Surely he took up our infirmities and carried our sorrows, yet we considered him stricken by God, smitten by him, and afflicted. But he was pierced for our transgressions, he was crushed for our iniquities; the punishment that brought us peace was upon him, and by his wounds we are healed. We all, like sheep, have gone astray, each of us has turned to his own way; and the Lord has laid on him the iniquity of us all. He was oppressed and afflicted-----For he was cut off from the land of the living; for the transgression of my people he was stricken. -----Yet it was the Lord's will to crush him and cause him to suffer, and though the Lord makes his life a guilt offering, he will see his offspring and prolong his days, and the will of the Lord will prosper in his hand. After the suffering of his soul, he will see the light of life and be satisfied; by his knowledge my righteous servant will justify many, and he will bear their iniquities----For he bore the sin of many and made intercession for the transgressors."

It is more than the human mind can comprehend to think that God made such a sacrifice as his own Holy and Sinless Son to die for such perverse, sinful and corrupt men who are capable of committing such awful acts as murder, rape, war, torture and having thoughts too wicked to mention, as well as committing the sin above all sins of turning their backs on the living God and making themselves the center of creation rather than God. (Romans 1:18-32)

The underlying issue in the fall of every sparrow is SIN and this is especially true in the suffering of Jesus Christ, the ultimate Sparrow who suffered and died for our sins. And the amazing thing about His suffering is that when He sees the outcome of that suffering He will say, "It was worth it!" "He shall see of the travail of his soul, and shall be satisfied." (Isaiah 53:11) *The Living Bible* clearly states the value of His suffering: "And when he sees all that is accomplished by the anguish of his soul, he shall be satisfied; and because of what he has experienced, my righteous Servant shall make many to be counted righteous before God, for he shall bear all their sins. Therefore I will give him the honors of one who is mighty and great, because he has poured out his soul unto death. He was counted as a sinner, and he bore the sins of many, and he pled with God for sinners." (Isaiah 53:11-12 LB)

This agony and suffering of Jesus on the cross is the untouched portrait of sin. There sin is exposed for the entire world to see, sin in its most graphic form! Sin--the underlying cause for all suffering and the fall of all sparrows.

It is through the sufferings of Christ that God the Father has accomplished the eternal salvation of all those who will repent of sin and accept him as their Savior. Just as surely as God used the sufferings of Jesus to accomplish our salvation he can use our sufferings to bless the lives of others and accomplish his eternal purpose. The love and mercy of God is interwoven with suffering so as to produce the fabric of salvation. <u>Due to the <u>nature of sin, suffering is inescapable</u></u>. It was inescapable for the Son of God if men were to be saved from sin, and it is certainly inescapable for us in this world.

Jesus was no stranger to pain, suffering, heartache and betrayal. He is referred to in Scripture as "a man of sorrows and acquainted with grief". Through it all he was a good steward of His suffering. May each of us also be good stewards of our suffering.

A Sparrow falls at Calvary, not by a boy with a BB gun in his hand, not only by the Jews or Pilate or the Roman soldiers who were present that fateful day, but by every man, for all have sinned! Yet the fall of that Sparrow (his death, burial, and resurrection) provides hope for all who believe in him, hope that they and their loved ones shall inherit a new heaven and a new earth wherein dwells righteousness where there shall be no more sin, no more suffering, no more death, no more sorrow, and no more tears—a place where sparrows never fall!

CHAPTER SEVEN

Through it all When Sparrows Fall

ROMANS 8:14-39

Many times when we ask the "Why?" question, we think God does not answer us! He does answer, it's just not the answer we want or expect. That is, his answer does not offer the solution to suffering to our satisfaction. God's answer to our suffering comes in many forms, such as, "My grace is sufficient for thee", or "My ways are not your ways", or "When you pass through the waters they shall not drown you or through the fire it shall not consume you".

Why doesn't God explain everything to us, especially suffering, so we can understand it? Perhaps he has and we have not been able to grasp it. Or perhaps we have refused to believe it or accept it. I wonder if God did explain it, even to our satisfaction, would that make any difference. Would a clear and concise explanation of suffering lessen the pain, heartache, and hurt? Also, would it lessen the sense of loss at the death of a loved one, or would it remove the disappointment and hurt of betrayal by a friend?

You see, when we ask the question "Why?" we are really asking God to stop the suffering, not just explain why it's happening. But instead of taking us out of our distressing circumstances our Father says, "I love you even though you are having a very difficult time, and to prove it I join you in your suffering. I know all about suffering. I sent my Son to be as you are, to live in a human body and endure all that you endure and much, much more!"

Jesus could say to each of us, "As a man I suffered. I learned obedience through suffering. (Though he were a Son, yet learned he obedience by the things which he suffered. Hebrews 5:8) I was tempted just as you are tempted. I faced trials. I hungered. I thirsted. I grew tired and weary. I endured sorrow. I cried. I endured physical pain. I hurt. I endured betrayal and denial. My own familiar friend lifted up his hand against me. My trusted follower denied that he even knew me. I know all about suffering. Today I walk with you in your 'fiery trials' of suffering just as I did with the three Hebrew children in their fiery furnace."

Our God is a very present help in time of trouble! "God is our refuge and strength, a very present help in trouble. Therefore will not we fear, though the earth be removed, and though the mountains be carried into the midst of the sea." (Psalm 46:1-2)

When sparrows fall God will be with us through it all. Many times we are not aware of his presence but he is there with words of encouragement and hope from unexpected sources. He is there with a word from friends, or family members, or the written Word of God, His own Word, the Holy Bible.

CONSIDER THE ENCOURAGEMENT AND HOPE FROM **FRIENDS**

There are friends, and then, there are friends. There are friends like those Job had, friends who sit in judgment; and then there are friends "who stick closer than a brother", friends who are a source of encouragement and strength through their understanding and counsel.

My friend Bill is such a friend. On one occasion in particular he called me at a time when I desperately needed help. It was at a time when Satan was attacking me from all sides. A black cloud of dismay was hovering over my head like a gathering tornado over an Oklahoma sky threatening to sweep down and wreck havoc on everything in its path. He had no way of knowing what was occurring in my life, yet he called that day and said, "Is there some particular reason I should call you today? It may simply be my imagination but it seems to me the Lord wanted me to call you and pray for you." Bill was God's messenger that day. On another occasion, I received a letter from him, which contained one of the "NUGGETS" he had written. It was very appropriate for my circumstances at the time. That kind of "stand-by-your-side" friendship is invaluable, especially when it comes at just the right time to strengthen you and encourage you.

Violent storms arise that threaten to shatter our lives, but there is a safe place to be in the midst of any storm. The Psalmist knew where to find a hiding place when the storms of life were raging. "Oh God, have pity, for I am trusting you! I will hide beneath the shadow of your wings until this storm is passed." (Psalm 57:1 LB) Not even the people of God are exempt from the storms of life. The Psalmist presents a pastoral scene, a farm picture, of a mother hen gathering her chickens under her wings in order to protect them from the storm. That's a picture of tranquility, peace, safety and protection! What more could a man want than to be "under the shadow of God's wings" during a powerful storm? No wonder the Psalmist said, "I'll just stay here in your presence until this storm is over." Not a bad place to be!

In Psalm 84:1-7, (LB) the Psalmist presents another picture of refuge and safety from the storms of life. It is the picture of a sparrow being invited by God to make His house his home. "Even the sparrows and swallows are welcome to come and nest among your altars…" Surely if the lowly sparrow can find a hiding place in the Tabernacle of God, we can find solace and contentment, safety and comfort in the presence of God during any storm. Those who join the sparrow in making

God's Temple their home, who want above all else to follow Him, even "When they walk through the Valley of Weeping it will become a place of springs where pools of blessing and refreshment collect after rains! They will grow constantly in strength and each of them is invited to meet with the Lord in Zion." (Psalm 84:6-7 LB)

Never underestimate the wisdom and power of God to send his messengers at a time when you need to "hear a word from the Lord". God sends a word of encouragement and hope from an unexpected source at a time when you need it most. In the very beginning of my ministry I was terrified at the thought of standing before people and speaking. Even when I was in High School I refused to read out loud when it came my turn to read in class. I knew if I tried my voice would quiver and my throat would become so tight I could not finish the paragraph. An older friend, who was called to preach about the same time I was, gave me advice which helped me greatly in my struggle with fear. The advice he gave me was this: "Keep your eyes on Jesus. As long as Peter kept his eyes on Jesus he was able to walk on water; only when he took his eyes off Jesus did he begin to sink. There is no storm or fear but what Jesus can keep you on top of it."

On another occasion when I was in college a beloved pastor, Dr. M. E. Ramay, gave me advice in the form of a challenge which constrained me to remain in college and complete my education, and for that matter remain in the ministry and continue in God's will for my life. Dr. Ramay said, in reply to my disillusionment with certain Christian leadership, "Don't let one man stand between you and God's will for your life." God used Dr. Ramay to encourage me and provide me with the insight I needed for that particular time and also for other similar times during my entire ministry.

Remember God is there to encourage you and give you hope through the counsel of friends.

CONSIDER THE ENCOURAGEMENT AND HOPE
FROM **FAMILY**

I was fortunate enough to have been born into a family with a legacy of love. It was a close knit family whose love for each other was founded upon the love of God. My knowledge of that love extended to the three previous generations (my great grandfather was an elder named Elijah) and continues through the following generations. It was this love and support from total family, their words of encouragement and their prayers, that provided much strength and understanding which could not be found from any other source.

Gerald, an older brother by birth and also a brother by the "new birth", gave me good counsel during my first pastorate out of seminary. Approximately a year into that pastorate, I became deeply discouraged and depressed, so much so that I called Gerald and drove over to Hominy to visit with him about the situation. We talked as we walked across the pasture where he kept his cattle. Gerald was a deep Christian and a very wise man and God used his advice and prayer that day to enable me to continue that pastorate for another three good years until the Lord called me to another church.

Another significant source of encouragement and hope came from Ruby, one of my three sisters. She gave me a small box filled with Scripture cards. The box was entitled: PRECIOUS THOUGHTS AND PROMISES FROM THE BIBLE. We read one of those cards at mealtime every day for thirty years until the box fell apart and the words grew dim. Those Scriptures were as necessary for our nurturing as the food on the table. They were a constant reminder of what Jesus said: "Man shall not live by bread alone, but by every word that comes from the mouth of God."(Matthew 4:4 ESV)

I always had the assurance that my brothers, sisters, father, mother, wife and three daughters were praying for me and for the Lord's blessing upon my ministry. Those prayers did more for me than they will ever know, and most assuredly more than I will ever know. I was most fortunate to have such a strong family prayer support.

No man was ever blessed by a more perfect "helpmate" than I! Anna stood by me, encouraged me, prayed for me and loved me more than any other, no matter what. She blessed my life and complimented my ministry in every way at all times. I could not have remained in the ministry had it not been for her insight, understanding, faithfulness and encouragement and prayers. On many occasions I drew from her own personal prayer promise based on I Peter 5:7 "Casting all your care upon him, for he careth for you." This promise is taken from the context of I Peter 5:6-11(LB) "If you will humble yourselves under the mighty hand of God, in his good time he will lift you up. Let him have all your worries and cares, for he is always thinking about you and watching everything that concerns you. Be careful--watch out for attacks from Satan, your great enemy. He prowls around like a hungry, roaring lion, looking for some victim to tear apart. Stand firm when he attacks. Trust the Lord; and remember that other Christians all around the world are going through these sufferings too. After you have suffered a little while, our God, who is full of kindness through Christ, will give you his eternal glory. He personally will come and pick you up, and set you firmly in place, and make you stronger than ever. To him be all power over all things, forever and ever. Amen."

It is my firm conviction that whatever I may have accomplished in life I owe it all to my wife, my family, my friends and God.

CONSIDER THE ENCOURAGEMENT AND HOPE FROM **GOD'S WORD**

During some of the darkest and most confusing times, God will provide encouragement and hope directly from his Word, the Holy Bible. Sometimes it will be a specific personal promise, a specific Scripture containing a direct personal promise from God for a particular and definite situation. That specific Scriptural promise will be pointed out to you and magnified by the Holy Spirit, and you will know that that promise is personal, as surely as if it were given to you and you alone for that particular time in your life. However, such specific promises are few and far between.

At other times there will be special personal promises in God's Word which the Holy Spirit will call to your attention and he will use those special Scriptures to assure you of God's presence, love, strength and guidance in your life. Of such scriptures, my sister Ruby used to say, "Right at the beginning of that verse it said, 'Ruby......'."

In addition to those specific personal promises and those special personal promises there are many general promises in God's Word that will encourage you and give you hope in the process of daily living.

SPECIFIC PERSONAL PROMISES

The first time I realized the Holy Spirit used a specific Scripture as a personal promise from God, was when I was trying to settle the issue of my salvation. After I was saved and had publicly accepted and confessed Jesus Christ as my personal Savior, I doubted my salvation for the next five or six years simply because I did not trust God's promise. I finally decided to settle, once and for all, the issue of my salvation. The Holy Spirit directed my attention to the Scripture which the pastor had me read the day I was saved. It was Romans 10:13, "For whosoever shall call upon the name of the Lord shall be saved." Then I said to God, "Ok, I'm going to call upon your name right now. I'm going to ask you to save me. I'm going to take you at your word that you will do what you said you would do." As I was praying this prayer the Holy Spirit said to me, not in audible words which my ears could hear, but in words which my soul could hear, "How many times have you prayed like this and asked me to save you?" I replied, "Many, many, many times." Then he replied, "I saved you the very first time you asked me. Is that not the promise I made in Romans 10:13? I promised I would save anyone who asked me." Then I said, "That's exactly what you promised! I believe you!" It was then I knew that all those years I had doubted my salvation, I was really saved. Since that evening when the Holy Spirit magnified God's promise in Romans 10:13, I have had the assurance of my salvation, an assurance based not upon my feelings, but based upon the specific promise of God in Romans 10:13.

The next such occasion came when I was struggling with whether or not God was calling me to preach. This particular occasion (there were several others) was the concluding and determining factor that confirmed God's call to me to preach His Word. It occurred in this manner: All of the churches in Osage County, Oklahoma, were engaged in revival meetings at the same time; they were called "Simultaneous Revivals". Before I left the house that evening I prayed and asked God to direct me to the church where He would have a definite word for me about preaching. As I drove down the highway I intended to go to a church in Cleveland, Oklahoma, a neighboring town. However, I was running late, and as I was leaving Hominy I changed my mind and drove to a small country church (Oak Hill Baptist Church) just a few miles outside of Hominy. By the time I arrived at the church they were singing the last verse of the last hymn. When they finished singing that verse the evangelist stood up to preach and began to read the passage of Scripture from which he would preach. The first three words out of his mouth were, "Preach the Word"! The Scripture he read was II Timothy 4:2, "Preach the word; be instant in season, out of season; reprove, rebuke, exhort with all longsuffering and doctrine."

That was God's clarion call for me to preach. There were other prayer experiences which contributed to my understanding of God's will for my life, but this specific Scripture confirmed God's call or command to preach his Word.

The third occasion when the Holy Spirit provided a specific Scriptural promise from God was when I attended Oklahoma Baptist University in Shawnee, Oklahoma. Before I graduated from Hominy High School I lived on a farm with my parents. Hominy was a small town with an approximate population of two thousand. Needless to say, I was intimidated by the size of Shawnee to say nothing of the size of the University. I felt completely out of place, totally insecure. It was at that point the Holy Spirit called my attention to Proverbs 3:5-6: "Trust in the LORD with all thine heart; and lean not unto thine own understanding. In all thy ways acknowledge him, and he shall direct thy paths." That promise sustained me, not only through Oklahoma Baptist University but also through Southwestern Baptist Theological Seminary as well as the rest of my life.

The fourth occasion for the Holy Spirit to magnify one of God's specific promises to me occurred while I was in Crippled Children's Hospital in Oklahoma City fighting my battle with polio. When my parents were killed in the car wreck the Holy Spirit again pointed out a particular promise from God: "Fear thou not; for I am with thee: be not dismayed, for I am thy God: I will strengthen thee; yea, I will help thee; yea, I will uphold thee with the right hand of my righteousness." (Isaiah 41:10) That promise was a constant source of encouragement and hope to me as I worked through the tragedy of my parent's death and the dreaded effects of polio. That promise became the focus of my pastoral ministry. I cannot recall the number of times I have fallen back on that Scripture during the dark days of my life, nor can I count the numerous times I have had opportunity to share that promise with others as they were dealing with the fall of sparrows in their own lives.

Another special occasion when I experienced the encouragement and hope from a specific promise from God's Word was when I resigned as pastor of my last church. With a complete lack of understanding on my part, after thirty years in the ministry the Lord assured me it was time to resign as pastor.

After my resignation I truly wondered what God had in store for me. For a preacher not to have a church to pastor is like a shepherd without sheep. It is quite disconcerting to say the least! Consequently, I became very distressed until the Holy Spirit came to my rescue with a brand new promise from God: "I know the plans I have for you, says the Lord. They are plans for good and not for evil, to give you a future and a hope." (Jeremiah 29:11 LB) The Holy Spirit lodged that promise in my heart. With that promise resting in my heart I knew, that even though I did not understand the situation, God was working out his plan for my life and it was for my good. I rested in the promise that my future was secure in the hands of God.

I believe with all of my heart that if you will listen to the Holy Spirit he will direct you to specific promises in the Word of God that will sustain you during the darkest hours and days of your life. At other times He will enable you to recall special and general promises in God's Word which will be a source of encouragement and hope during the process of daily living.

SPECIAL PROMISES

At this point I want to share with you some special promises from God, which have blessed my soul and whispered sweet peace to my heart during the course of my life.

1. John 14:27 "Peace I leave with you, my peace I give unto you: not as the world giveth give I unto you. Let not your heart be troubled, neither let it be afraid."

   If you will allow those words, from the lips of Jesus our Savior, to flow freely back and forth in your heart and mind you will discover the wonderful peace of God even in the midst of your daily problems, troubles, and fears. Permit the Holy Spirit to fill your soul with His divine peace.

2. Psalm 51:10-12 "Create in me a clean heart, O God; and renew a right spirit within me. Cast me not away from thy presence; and take not thy Holy Spirit from me. Restore unto me the joy of thy salvation; and uphold me with thy free Spirit."

    When you are discouraged in body and soul, if you will pray this prayer and submit your will to the Father's will, the Holy Spirit will give you a new perspective and renew your outlook on life.

3. Psalm 56:3-4 "What time I am afraid, I will trust in thee. In God I will praise his word, in God I have put my trust; I will not fear what flesh can do unto me."

    All of us become fearful at times. When those fears begin to plague your thoughts it is time to confront them, deal with them, and do so with faith in God. Confront them one by one, confirming your faith in God by saying with the Psalmist, "In the very midst of my fears I am trusting God." Trust him no matter what!

4. Psalm 46:1-2 "God is our refuge and strength, a very present help in trouble. Therefore will not we fear, though the earth be removed, and though the mountains be carried into the midst of the sea."

    Whenever you are in trouble, remember, God is with you, helping you and giving you strength.

5. Romans 8:37-39 "In all these things we are more than conquerors through Him that loved us. For I am persuaded, that neither death, nor life, nor angels, nor principalities, nor

powers, nor things present, nor things to come, nor height, nor depth, nor any other creature, shall be able to separate us from the love of God, which is in Christ Jesus our Lord."

Life can be very disturbing and enemies may abound; however, no matter what happens, no matter how dire the circumstance, remember this: Nothing can separate you from God's love! Rest in the assurance that God's love for you never diminishes!

6. Isaiah 26:3 "Thou wilt keep him in perfect peace, whose mind is stayed on thee: because he trusteth in thee. Trust ye in the Lord forever: for in the Lord JEHOVAH is everlasting strength."

One of the most difficult things in life is to stay focused on God. Practice the presence of God and experience the peace of God, "the peace that passes all understanding."

7. Isaiah 41:10 "Fear thou not; for I am with thee: be not dismayed; for I am thy God: I will strengthen thee; yea, I will help thee; yea, I will uphold thee with the right hand of my righteousness."

Through the years God has been and will be faithful to do just that. Count on it!

Those are the special promises of God which have sustained me through the years. My prayer is that they may enrich your life and be a source of blessing to you as they have been to me.

Through it all, when sparrows fall, it has been God's Word that has sustained me. Truly as Jesus said, "Man shall not live by bread alone but by every word of God."

GENERAL PROMISES OF GOD

Following are a few of the general promises of God found in the Bible, promises which are a source of encouragement and hope to all who believe. One of the reasons we should saturate our mind and heart with the Word of God is, that by doing so, it enables the Holy Spirit to call his promises to our attention and magnify them in such a way that we will trust God even when sparrows fall.

I have found the following samples of God's promises to be a taste of honey along the way, which the Holy Spirit can use to make the bitter things of life a little sweeter:

"The law of the Lord is perfect, converting the soul: the testimony of the Lord is sure, making wise the simple. The statutes of the Lord are right, rejoicing the heart: the commandment of the Lord is pure, enlightening the eyes. The fear of the Lord is clean, enduring forever: the judgments of the Lord are true and righteous altogether. More to be desired are they than gold, yea, than much fine gold: sweeter also than honey and the honeycomb. Moreover by them is thy servant warned: and in keeping of them there is great reward." (Psalm 19:7-11) "How sweet are thy words unto my taste! yea, sweeter than honey to my mouth!" (Psalm 119:103)

The Promise of God's Presence

"Be strong! Be courageous! Do not be afraid of them! For the Lord your God will be with you. He will neither fail you nor forsake you." (Deuteronomy 31:6 LB)

The Promise of God's Power

"Hast thou not known? Hast thou not heard, that the everlasting God, the Lord, the Creator of the ends of the earth, fainteth not, neither is weary? there is no searching of his understanding. He giveth power to the faint; and to them that have no might he increaseth strength. Even the youths shall faint and be weary, and the young men shall utterly fall: But they that wait upon the Lord shall renew their strength; they shall mount up with wings as eagles; they shall run, and not be weary; and they shall walk, and not faint." (Isaiah 40:28-31)

The Promise of God's Love

"Who shall separate us from the love of Christ? Shall tribulation, or distress, or persecution, or famine, or nakedness, or peril, or sword? Nay, in all these things we are more than conquerors through him that loved us. For I am persuaded, that neither death, nor life, nor angels, nor principalities, nor powers, nor things present, nor things to come, nor height, nor depth, nor any other creature, shall be able to separate us from the love of God, which is in Christ Jesus our Lord." (Romans 8:35, 37-39)

The Promise of God's Peace

"Peace I leave with you, my peace I give unto you: not as the world giveth, give I unto you. Let not your heart be troubled, neither let it be afraid." (John 14:27)

The Promise of God's Comfort

"Praise be to the God and Father of our Lord Jesus Christ, the Father of compassion and the God of all comfort, who comforts us in all our troubles, so that we can comfort those in any trouble with the comfort we ourselves have received from God" (2 Corinthians 1:3-4 NIV).

There are many other general promises in God's Word which the Holy Spirit can apply to your need, promises which will enable you to face the issue before you at any given time, and work through it to acceptance and victory. Truly, as Jesus said, "Man shall not live by bread alone but by every word that comes from the mouth of God". (Matthew 4:4 ESV)

Be assured, when a sparrow falls, God is there in and through the support of the family, the affirmation of friends, the total ministry of the Holy Spirit, and the assurance and power of his written Word!

Through it all, when sparrows fall, it has been God's Word that has sustained me! Through it all, when sparrows fall, it can be God's Word that sustains you!

CHAPTER EIGHT

Lessons to be Learned

Through it all, when sparrows fall there are lessons to be learned and a life remains to be lived, although life is permanently altered by the fall of each sparrow and will never be the same again. The fall of a sparrow demands an adjustment to the life remaining on this earth. Making this adjustment from the way life was, to the way life now is, is most difficult.

Here are a few concepts which have been beneficial to me in dealing with the fall of sparrows. My prayer is that they may help you in dealing with the fall of sparrows in your own life.

TEARS ARE HEALING

"Sorrow is better than laughter: for by the sadness of the countenance the heart is made better" (Ecclesiastes 7:3). To some degree The Living Bible Paraphrased clarifies the King James Version of this Scripture: "Sorrow is better than laughter, for sadness has a refining influence on us." There is cleansing power in crying. Crying is therapeutic; it is cathartic; it is beneficial to the heart. There is a time to weep and there is a time to laugh. (Ecclesiastes 3:4) When sparrows fall is a time to weep.

GOD'S GRACE IS SUFFICIENT

"My grace is sufficient for you." (2 Corinthians 12:9 NIV) Grace is God's sufficiency to handle your losses and sorrows as well as your sins. Sometimes God delivers, but sometimes He gives grace to endure.

SUFFERING IS A NECESSITY OF LIFE

"Though he give you the bread of adversity and water of affliction, yet he will be with you to teach you—with your own eyes you will see your Teacher." (Isaiah 30:20 LB) Bread and water sustain life. Man cannot live without bread and water. Can it be that the bread of adversity and the water of affliction are also essential to life? At least there are lessons to be learned from suffering and God himself is our teacher. "It is good for me that I have been afflicted; that I might learn thy statutes." (Psalm 119:71)

SUFFERING IS AN OPPORTUNITY FOR STEWARDSHIP

Don't waste your sorrows. Don't waste your suffering. Don't waste your sorrows and sufferings on self-pity; rather be a good steward of both.

We are to be good stewards of our sorrows as well as our talents, finances, resources and every other aspect of life. Suffering has its place in our lives. God uses suffering to bless our lives and the lives of others as they see our suffering. God himself is a good steward of suffering. "And we know that in all things God works for the good of those who love him, who have been called according to his purpose." (Romans 8:28 NIV) We should be good stewards of suffering as well. We should use our suffering for good just as God used the suffering of

Jesus—to honor God and help others. If out of the suffering and dying of Jesus Christ God brings eternal good to me and makes it available to all humanity, can he not also bring good to us and others out of our suffering and dying? God as the Divine Alchemist is able to produce good from suffering.

GOD USES SUFFERING

1. To <u>mature us in the faith</u>—"We can rejoice, too, when we run into problems and trials for we know that they are good for us—they help us learn to be patient. And patience develops strength of character in us and helps us trust God more each time we use it until finally our hope and faith are strong and steady. Then, when that happens, we are able to hold our heads high no matter what happens and know that all is well, for we know how dearly God loves us, and we feel this warm love everywhere within us because God has given us the Holy Spirit to fill our hearts with his love."(Romans 5:3-5 LB)

2. To <u>equip us to minister</u>—"What a wonderful God we have—he is the Father of our Lord Jesus Christ, the source of every mercy, and the one who so wonderfully comforts and strengthens us in our hardships and trials. And why does he do this? So that when others are troubled, needing our sympathy and encouragement, we can pass on to them this same help and comfort God has given us. You can be sure that the more we undergo sufferings for Christ, the more he will shower us with his comfort and encouragement."(2 Corinthians 1:3-5 LB)

3. To <u>encourage us to trust him</u>—"But Jesus the Son of God is our great High Priest who has gone to heaven itself to help us; therefore let us never stop trusting him. This High Priest of ours understands our weaknesses, since he had the same temptations we do, though he never once gave way to them and sinned. So let us come boldly to the very throne of God

81

and stay there to receive his mercy and to find grace to help us in our times of need." (Hebrews 4:14-16 LB)

4. To <u>remind us of his sovereign purposes</u>—"As he was walking along, he saw a man blind from birth. 'Master,' his disciples asked him, 'why was this man born blind? Was it a result of his own sins or those of his parents?' 'Neither', Jesus answered. 'But to demonstrate the power of God." (John 9:1-3 LB)

Joseph said to his brothers who had sold him into Egyptian slavery, "God has sent me here to keep you and your families alive, so that you will become a great nation. Yes, it was God who sent me here, not you!"(Genesis 45:7-8 LB) "As far as I am concerned, God turned into good what you meant for evil, for he brought me to this high position I have today so that I could save the lives of many people."(Genesis 50:20 LB)

5. To <u>teach us to be obedient</u>—even Jesus learned obedience through suffering—"And even though Jesus was God's Son, he had to learn from experience what it was like to obey, when obeying meant suffering."(Hebrews 5:8 LB)

6. To <u>reveal the Glory of Jesus Christ</u>—"But when Jesus heard about it he said, The purpose of his illness is not death, but for the glory of God. I, the Son of God, will receive glory from this situation."(John 11:4 LB)

7. To <u>develop within us a "but if not" kind of faith</u>—When the three Hebrew children were threatened with being thrown into a fiery furnace if they refused to bow down to the image of the King of Babylon, they said, "Our God whom we serve is able to deliver us from the burning fiery furnace, --<u>But if not,</u> be it known unto thee, O king, that we will not serve thy gods, nor worship the golden image which thou hast set up." (Daniel 3:17-18)

Why are some of God's servants delivered from the fire, but others are burned at the stake? Why are some eaten by wild beasts yet others are kept safe even in the lions' den? Why are some delivered from prison while others are beheaded? If you can answer such questions sufficiently to soothe the sorrows of others, you have reached a level of spiritual maturity which most never attain. However, for all, the following poem by Alan Redpath provides a perspective worth considering:

> "There is nothing--
> no circumstance,
> no trouble,
> no testing,
> that can ever touch me until, first of all,
> it has gone past God
> and past Christ,
> right through to me.
> If it has come that far,
> it has come with great purpose,
> which I may not understand at the moment;
> but as I refuse to become panicky,
> as I lift up my eyes to Him
> and accept it as coming from the throne of God
> for some great purpose of blessing to my own heart,
> no sorrow will disturb me,
> no trial will ever disarm me,
> no circumstance will cause me to fret,
> for I shall REST in the joy of what my Lord is.
> That is the REST of victory."
> ---- Alan Redpath

God is still in control even when things seem out of control. Without God's permission not even Satan can do anything to harm you. (Job 1:8-12; 2:1-7) Dietrich Bonhoeffer, who died for his faith during the reign of Hitler, wrote: "I am in God's hands, not in men's. No earthly power can touch us without His will, and dangers and distresses can only drive us closer to Him."

GOD HIMSELF IS OUR REFUGE

During the storms of life the only safe haven is God. "The eternal God is thy refuge, and underneath are the everlasting arms."(Deuteronomy 33:27) "God is our refuge and strength, a very present help in trouble."(Psalm 46:1) "I long, yes, faint with longing to be able to enter your courtyard and come near to the Living God. Even the sparrows and swallows are welcome to come and nest among your altars and there have their young, O Lord of heaven's armies, my King and my God! How happy are those who can live in your Temple, singing your praises. Happy are those who are strong in the Lord, who want above all else to follow your steps. When they walk through the Valley of Weeping it will become a place of springs where pools of blessing and refreshment collect after rains! They will grow constantly in strength and each of them is invited to meet with the Lord in Zion."(Psalm 84:2-7 LB) "The Lord is close to those whose hearts are breaking; he rescues those who are humbly sorry for their sins. The good man does not escape all troubles—he has them too. But the Lord helps him in each and every one." (Psalm 34:18-19 LB)

GOD IS SOVEREIGN

Your concept of God, your understanding of Him, the kind of God you believe Him to be—his power, his purpose, his character, his attributes—will affect every aspect of your life! It will determine your ethics, your sense of right and wrong. It will determine your relationship and attitude toward others—in the family, the community, the church, the government, the world, and on the job. It will determine your response to every situation, whether it be good or bad, joyful or sad, success or failure. It will even affect your prayer life and your faith and trust in God himself!

Is your God a sovereign God? Is He the Supreme Ruler of the universe? Is He in absolute control of everything? Is He at liberty to act according to His character, or must He conform to your wishes or someone else's wishes? If He does not act the way you think He should, do you still trust Him?

There are only two cosmic powers in the universe: God and Satan. God is good. Satan is evil. However, Satan can do nothing without God's permission. God is sovereign! God allows Satan limited latitude in his activity. In his sovereignty God gives Satan permission to inflict suffering; however, He restricts him as to how much suffering he can inflict at a given time. Satan secured God's consent to strike Job with extensive suffering and consequently Job experienced the fall of many sparrows. One after another they fell: his oxen, his asses, his sheep, his camels, his servants, his sons and daughters, and his own health also. Before Job had time to process the fall of the first sparrow, the second sparrow fell; then the third and the fourth until Job had lost everything he loved most, and found himself sitting on the ash heap scraping the scabs from his infected, sickly, wasted body. There he sat in the midst of his suffering, no doubt wondering, "Why? Why has all this befallen me?"

God gave Satan permission to cause the fall of all of Job's sparrows; but in each instance God informed Satan that he could only go so far and no farther. "The Lord said to Satan, 'Very well, then, everything he has is in your hands, but on the man himself do not lay a finger". At a later point, "The Lord said to Satan, 'Very well then, he is in your hands; but you must spare his life'." (Job 1:12; 2:6 NIV)

When it comes to the subject of suffering, the suffering of Job provides an insight which no other book in the Bible provides. In the beginning of the Book of Job, we are permitted to see and hear something, which Job and his friends are not allowed to know. They are kept in the dark as to what is occurring in Heaven. Something is transpiring in Heaven of which the reader is aware, but Job and his friends are not. They are totally ignorant of the conversation between God and Satan; yet that conversation will directly affect each of their lives!

Satan is questioning Job's faith, his motive, and his integrity, but God has complete confidence in Job; consequently, he gives Satan permission to put Job to the test.

I cannot help but wonder how much of our own suffering comes from the same source as Job's. At least, we are provided the insight of God's conversation with Satan, and we are aware that sometimes God gives Satan permission to bring suffering into our lives, as he did Job's.

When God permits suffering to enter our lives we can rest assured he has his own purposes, whether he lets us in on it or not; and we can also rest assured that He will bring good out of our suffering, which will glorify him and bless others. "And we know that in all things God works for the good of those who love him, who have been called according to his purpose" (Romans 8:28 NIV).

Why doesn't God explain everything, especially suffering? Perhaps he has, and the problem is we have been unable to understand or accept it. But even if God did explain it to our satisfaction would that lessen the pain, or the sorrow, or the sense of loss at the death of a loved one, or the disappointment and hurt of betrayal by a friend? For that matter, does God even owe us an explanation? Perhaps not! For those of us who would find fault with God, Paul asks a very pertinent question in Romans 9:20-21 (paraphrased): "But indeed, O man, who are you to reply against God? Will the thing formed say to him who formed it, 'Why have you made me like this?' Does not the potter have power over the clay, from the same lump to make one vessel for honor and another for dishonor?"

Even though God has his own purposes that he may or may not share with us, that does not diminish his love for us nor does it lessen our responsibility to maintain the purity of our faith, our motive, and our integrity. Whether we are permitted to be in on God's plans or not, God still remains true to his character as God. We must permit God to be God in our personal lives as well as in all other realms, otherwise he is not God.

What is held in question here (Job's suffering) is not the character of God but the character of Job. The question is, "How will he react to his suffering?" Will he "curse God and die" or will he "maintain his integrity"? The purity of Job's motive for trusting and serving God has been called into question by Satan: "Doth Job serve thee for naught?"

Can you accept the fact that God and Satan had a private conversation of which Job knew nothing, yet Job had to live with the consequences? Job had to respond to each of those tragedies without knowing anything at all about the agreement between God and Satan. Can you accept the fact that Job is the one on trial here, not God? The question is not what will God do for Job in his sufferings, but what will Job do in his sufferings. Will Job trust God through his sufferings or will he give-up on God and do as his wife urged him to do, "curse God and die"?

Are you able to accept the total and absolute Sovereignty of God? Can you believe that nothing, absolutely nothing, can occur without God's permission? Not even one single sparrow can fall without His permission. Can you go so far as to believe that not a single murder, rape, war, robbery, disease, deformity, life or death can occur without God's permission? Strange as it may seem, there is peace and hope and assurance in that truth, because of who God is! "Oh, what a wonderful God we have! How great are his wisdom and knowledge and riches! How impossible it is for us to understand his decisions and his methods! For who among us can know the mind of the Lord? Who knows enough to be his counselor and guide?" (Romans 11:33-34 LB)

God is still sovereign, even in the midst of all our sufferings. There are times we think God should resign and let us take over. However, God does not run his world the way we think He should, but according to his own character and purpose. He made that plain in Isaiah 55:8-9 "For my thoughts are not your thoughts, neither are your ways my ways, saith the Lord. For as the heavens are higher than the earth, so are my ways higher than your ways, and my thoughts than your thoughts." We should keep in mind that God also said, "I know the plans I have for you; they are plans for good and not for evil, to give you a future and a hope."(Jeremiah 29:11 LB)

Job had to face the human dilemma of suffering without knowledge of God's deal with Satan. How many other factors, of which we know nothing, enter into the equation of suffering? When things don't add up like we think they should, perhaps we have miscalculated the meaning and purpose of suffering because we do not know all the factors that figure into the equation. In our struggle to settle this issue of suffering, let us stand firm with Job and say, "Though he slay me, yet will I trust in him"! (Job 13:15)

CHAPTER NINE

The Final Sparrow

As I have reflected on all the fallen sparrows in my life I have come to the inevitable conclusion that the last sparrow to fall in my life will be me. The final sparrow to fall in your life is you.

Death is inevitable! "It is appointed unto men once to die, but after this the judgment."(Hebrews 9:27) Death began in the Garden of Eden when Adam and Eve disobeyed God and ate the forbidden fruit. "And the Lord God commanded the man, saying, Of every tree of the garden thou mayest freely eat: but of the tree of the knowledge of good and evil, thou shalt not eat of it: for in the day that thou eatest thereof thou shalt surely die." (Genesis 2:16-17) "Wherefore, as by one man sin entered into the world, and death by sin; and so death passed upon all men, for that all have sinned."(Romans 5:12) Death is part of God's plan, and it is inevitable!

In the fifth chapter of Genesis the Bible sets forth the inevitability of death for every man with the recurring phrase: "and he died". Regardless of how many years each man lived, he died. The only person of whom it was not said, "and he died" was Enoch and the only explanation for this exception is the fact that Enoch walked with God. "Enoch walked with God; then he was no more, because God took him away."(Genesis 5:24 NIV) This truth gives us hope of victory over death, but only for those who prepare for it.

Preparing for this inevitable event requires forethought and action. It requires making plans for the disposition of all your earthly possessions including your body. (See Appendix I) Of much more importance eternally is making plans for your soul and then carrying out those plans. It is imperative that I repeat—**each person is responsible for his own soul.** (See Appendix II)

Although the disposition of your material assets is extremely important the disposition of your soul is the most important decision of your life! At this very moment unless you have already placed your soul into the hands of God for safe-keeping, your soul is in the hands of Satan; you are a child of his and you are in Satan's family. Unless you are born again and become a child of God through faith in Jesus Christ you will spend eternity in Hell with Satan and those who belong to him.

Due to the issue of sin we are all alienated from God. Upon our physical birth we were born into this world as children of Satan. One day Jesus was speaking with a group known as Pharisees, a very religious group who refused to believe that Jesus was the Son of God, and he said to them, "Ye are of your father, the devil, and the lusts of your father ye will do. He was a murderer from the beginning, and abode not in the truth, because there is no truth in him. When he speaketh a lie, he speaketh of his own: for he is a liar, and the father of it. And because I tell you the truth, ye believe me not. He that is of God heareth God's words: ye therefore hear them not, because ye are not of God."(John 8:44-45, 47)

We were born with a sinful nature and we must be born again spiritually, if we are to have a new nature, a godly nature that is capable of worshiping and serving God. When Jesus was talking with Nicodemus, a ruler of the Jews, he said to him, "Verily, verily, I say unto thee, Except a man be born again, he cannot see the Kingdom of God. That which is born of the flesh is flesh; and that which is born of the Spirit is spirit. Marvel not that I said unto thee, Ye must be born again. For God so loved the world, that he gave his only begotten Son, that whosoever believeth in him should not perish, but have everlasting life. For God sent not his Son into the world to condemn the world; but that the world through him might be saved. He that believeth on him is not condemned: but he that believeth not is condemned already, because he hath not believed in the name of the only begotten Son of God." (John 3:3, 6-7, 16-18)

To be born into the family of God is a matter of faith, "So then faith cometh by hearing, and hearing by the word of God."(Romans 10:17) "Whosoever believeth that Jesus is the Christ is born of God."(I John 5:1) "Whatsoever is born of God overcometh the world: and this is the victory that overcometh the world, even our faith. Who is he that overcometh the world, but he that believeth that Jesus is the Son of God?"(I John 5:4-5) "This is the record, that God hath given to us eternal life, and this life is in his Son. He that hath the Son hath life; and he that hath not the Son of God hath not life. These things have I written unto you that believe on the name of the Son of God; that ye may know that ye have eternal life..." (I John 5:11-13)

If you are not a child of God and you want to be and you want to place your soul, your life, your future into his hands for safe-keeping, then tell him the desires of your heart. "But what saith it? The word is nigh thee, even in thy mouth, and in thy heart: that is, the word of faith, which we preach; that if thou shalt confess with thy mouth the Lord Jesus and shalt believe in thine heart that God hath raised him from the dead, thou shalt be saved...For whosoever shall call upon the name of the Lord shall be saved." (Romans 10:8-9, 13)

Death is inescapable! It is the fall of the final sparrow for each of us. Death is one appointment we shall all keep and we shall not be a moment late. We shall meet Death at the appointed hour, and then the Judgment! "And as it is appointed unto men once to die, but after this the Judgment: So Christ was once offered to bear the sins of many; and unto them that look for him shall he appear the second time without sin unto salvation." (Hebrews 9:27-28) If you want to make proper disposition of your soul then ask Jesus Christ to be your Savior, then when you keep your appointment with death, you will be able to say with Jesus, "Father, into thy hands I commend my spirit."(Luke 23:46)

Beware of an unrealistic utopian faith! An irrational faith or unrealistic faith is one that believes life is all smiles and no tears, all health and no sickness, all riches and no poverty, all holiness and no sin, all ups and no downs, all positive and no negative, all joy and no sadness, all play and no work, all gain and no loss, all life and no death.

A realistic faith deals with life as it is, not as we think it should be! A realistic faith must face the Cross of Jesus before it can experience the resurrection; it must first face death before it can experience the empty tomb. A realistic faith must face the enemy on the battlefield before it can experience victory. A realistic faith must embrace Jesus Christ as Lord and Savior to be victorious over the realities of life and sin and death.

A realistic faith takes into consideration the total human experience from life to death, health to sickness, success to failure, prosperity to poverty, peace to persecution, and evil to good. A realistic faith deals with life as it is and carries the believer through the human experience to victory. This is the victory that overcomes the world, even our faith. "For whatsoever is born of God overcometh the world: and this is the victory that overcometh the world, even our faith. Who is he that overcometh the world, but he that believeth that Jesus is the Son of God?"(I John 5:4-5)

If you have invited Jesus Christ into your life to take care of your sin problem as well as all the affairs of your life, and if you are enjoying fellowship with him through his Word, then you have all the resources you need to face the fall of each sparrow in your life, as well as your own fall—and fall you will—for sparrows do fall. However, not a single sparrow can fall without the permission and presence of our Heavenly Father! I join the apostle Paul in saying: I know the one in whom I trust, and I am sure that he is able to safely guard all (soul, family, friends, finances, and future) that I have given him until the day of his return. (II Timothy 1:12 LB)

Conclusion

My solution, with reference to the "why" of the fall of sparrows, is simply this: **Trust!**

Trust in the all sufficiency and loving-kindness of a purposeful God who revealed Himself in Jesus Christ through the Bible. That is the only way to face life with all of its realities. God's revelation of Himself is the only sustaining reality of life.

Through trust in God lies the hope of the world and the only satisfying solution to suffering and the appropriate perspective of the "why" question.

My eternal, settled position is this: I trust God without reservation. Biblical faith results in trust, the kind of trust which becomes a bedrock commitment to the character of God; the kind of trust exhibited by Job when he said, "Though He slay me, yet will I trust in him"! (Job 13:15)

I do not understand everything God has done and said, nor do I understand everything which he allows to take place; but where understanding ends, faith and trust continue! That is as it should be because God's logic goes beyond man's logic or ability to think. "For my thoughts are not your thoughts, neither are your ways my ways, declares the Lord, As the heavens are higher than the earth, so are my ways higher than your ways and my thoughts than your thoughts." (Isaiah 55:8-9 NIV) "No eye has seen, no ear has heard, no mind has conceived what God has prepared for those who love him." (I Corinthians 2:9 NIV)

There is a "fellowship of suffering" in which people bear one another's burdens; it is the fellowship of sharing in Christ's sufferings (Philippians 3:10 LB). Join this fellowship, and walk with the victorious Jesus "who for the joy that was set before him endured the cross, despising the shame, and is set down at the right hand of the throne of God."(Hebrews 12:2).

Come, walk with me, and together we shall walk with God throughout the rest of our journey until we arrive at our Heavenly home, the one prepared for us by Jesus himself, where we shall join our Heavenly Father, family and friends in that place **<u>where sparrows never fall!</u>**

Scripture

"Are not two sparrows sold for a farthing? And one of them shall not fall on the ground without your Father. Fear ye not therefore, ye are of more value than many sparrows."
Matthew 10:29, 31

"And God shall wipe away all tears from their eyes; and there shall be no more death, neither sorrow, nor crying, neither shall there be any more pain: for the former things are passed away."
Revelation 21:4

Appendix 1

MAN'S PLAN OF PREPARATION

Let's look briefly at plans for disposing of all of our material possessions, including the body in which we live; then we will consider the disposition of our soul which is far more important than the disposition of material things. "For what shall it profit a man, if he shall gain the whole world, and lose his own soul?"(Mark 8:36)

It is essential for you to give detailed consideration to the following issues and act upon these decisions in a timely manner. Procrastination in preparing for death could very well mean allowing someone else to make those decisions for you when you become incapacitated or die. Some issues to consider are:

- A Revocable Trust, which would authorize the distribution of your monetary accounts, investments, retirement accounts, insurance policies, real estate property, and personal property.

- An Advanced Directive for health care, which would consist of a Durable Power of Attorney, the appointment of a Health Care Proxy, a Living Will and Anatomical Gifts, if any, and a legal paper designating your HIPPA Representatives giving them access to your medical condition and records.

- A Simple Will (if one cannot afford a Trust or feel the need for one) should include the above suggestions.

- A Document listing the location of vital and personal papers, such as Social Security Card, Medicare Card, Credit Cards, Burial Lots, Funeral arrangements, Marriage License, Deeds, Car

Titles, Trust Documents, Investments with account numbers, Insurance policies, etc., plus the names, addresses, and phone numbers of all contact persons.

The above are the broad considerations necessary if you wish your final days upon this earth to be as you would like for them to be and the distribution of your material assets to be of your choosing.

Appendix II

GOD'S PLAN OF SALVATION

God's plan of salvation is his Son, Jesus Christ!

If you have Him you have salvation!

If you do not have Him you do not have salvation!

"He who has the Son has life; he who does not have the Son of God does not have life." (I John 5:12 NIV)

"Jesus answered, 'I am the way and the truth and the life. No one comes to the Father except through me.'" (John 14:5 NIV)

"Salvation is found in no one else, for there is no other name under heaven given to men by which we must be saved." (Acts 4:12 NIV)

"For God so loved the world that he gave his one and only Son, that whoever believes in him shall not perish but have eternal life.... Whoever believes in him is not condemned, but whoever does not believe stands condemned already because he has not believed in the name of God's one and only Son." (John 3:16, 18 NIV)

"Yet to all who received him, to those who believed in his name, he gave the right to become the children of God." (John 1:12 NIV)

If you do not know the Heavenly Father who sees the fall of every sparrow, you can know him. Jesus wants to be your Savior. He wants to save you from sin—its penalty, its power, and ultimately its presence. Would you like to receive Him as your Lord and Savior? If so, invite Him into your life just as you would invite a guest into your home. He is standing at the door of your heart, and He is saying, "Here I am. I stand at the door and knock. If anyone hears my voice and opens the door, I will come in and eat with him, and he with me." (Revelation 3:20 NIV) In other words Jesus is offering to come into your life and live! Will you invite Him in? You may use your own words or pray the following prayer:

Dear Heavenly Father, please forgive me for being a sinner and save me. I do believe that Jesus died for my sins and that you raised Him from the dead. Now, Lord Jesus, I open the door of my heart and invite you into my life. Amen.

According to God's Word, "Everyone who calls on the name of the Lord will be saved." (Romans 10:13 NIV)

May the Lord bless you as you walk with Him day by day.

LaVergne, TN USA
09 January 2010
169438LV00004B/8/P